HOPE FOR AUTISM

The 262 Billion Dollar Solution:
Improving Medical, Academic, and
Behavior Needs

JAMIE JUAREZ MELILLO, M.S.
DOCTOR OF EDUCATION CANDIDATE

—WITH—
DOMINIC S. JUAREZ, "THE TYPER"

FOREWORD BY: DR. SHAZIA HYDER, M.D.

Contents

INTRODUCTION..1

CHAPTER 1: Autism: My Life, My Passion.............................5

CHAPTER 2: The Current, Flawed Definition of Autism 13

CHAPTER 3: The Autism Brain and Immune System
Connection 27

CHAPTER 4: The Autism Brain, Behavior, and Learning
Connection 53

CHAPTER 5: Empirically Supported Treatments and
Promising Practices...67

CHAPTER 6: Applied Behavioral Analysis in Autism.......................79

CHAPTER 7: What Is Cognitive Behavioral Therapy 97

CHAPTER 8: Assistive Augmentative Technology's
Role in Autism...101

CHAPTER 9: The Role for ESP, Savants, and True Learning
Potentials in Autism 109

CHAPTER 10: What is the Rapid Prompting Training's
"Your Child Can Type"?...................................119

CHAPTER 11: What is an Exemplar Comprehensive Evidence-Based Program? 137

APPENDIX: A Reference Guide to Common Behavioral 175

ABOUT THE AUTHORS 187

Hope for Autism is dedicated to my amazingly strong, blessed children Danielle, Dominic, Devin, and Daliah Juarez. I would do anything for you, including temporarily sacrificing my own sanity to achieve transparent peace, hope, and freedom for you in this world striving for a loving humanity. It is in honor of all the families, students, patients, therapists, teachers, aides, doctors, attorneys, firemen, police, military, nurses, churches, mosques, temples, universities, investors, donors, and technology experts who benevolently dedicated their time and effort to our family against all odds in effort to model justice and liberty for all.

Introduction

Hope for Autism is about an 18-year professional and personal journey against all odds to prove that my autism-diagnosed and vaccine-injured son was and is, in fact, able to learn with quality, ethically based services. Our painful journey attempts to expose the aggressive victimization of corporate pharmaceutical companies and big-government greed that creates and isolates those with mental and biological illnesses. Our love for humanity led to sacrificing our minds, bodies, and souls in hope of truth, justice, and liberty for all in such a way that many haven't yet comprehended. We pray our family, our friends, and the world at large ultimately understand our self-sacrifice.

My son Dominic was born typical. When he became vaccine-injured we sought biomedical services, applied behavior analysis, speech therapy, and occupational therapy, all of which were automatically denied. As this was happening, I was simultaneously learning about how autistic children learn and communicate differently than neurotypical children. Over a one-week period when he was three years old, I figured out how to teach him his alphabet, numbers, and name. The results proved that with a modified approach my son could read, spell, and type.

Despite severe damage to his speech and pointing skills, Dominic could still match, engage in puzzles, and manipulate DVDs and cell phones quickly. I began purchasing 3D educational materials for him to demonstrate that he was still capable of learning and communicating despite his extreme behavior impedances. The autistic brain appeared to see better in 3D than in 2D; 2D is traditional paper, pencil, paperback books whereas 3D are visual graphics commonly observed to stimulate different areas of the brain. I started developing 3D worksheets, 3D visual graphic representations, and purchasing 3D manipulations such as Leap Frog rather than traditional teaching materials.

Social services, insurance companies, and school districts observed my demonstration of Dominic's capabilities and those of my patients and students, but they still denied Dominic's services and accused me of being crazy. Other families were being automatically denied also, despite this knowledge and laws in place to assist the children. I became driven to learn about the brain, behavior, education, and laws to help my son and others diagnosed erroneously with autism and mental retardation. With all this knowledge and utter feelings of helplessness for my child, his siblings, and the community at large, I founded our own non-profits to provide all the needed services for my son and others in the community.

I now knew without a doubt that children with autism could learn to communicate. They just learned differently due to this newly impacted type of brain. My ability to teach my own son grew quickly to helping hundreds around the country. Today, I relentlessly advocate for everyone impacted around the world through my Rosenhan-Juarez Experiment while at USC's Global Executive Policy Program validating Hope for Autism's research.

We are so very excited for you to read this training manual that has successfully settled over 30 million dollars in wrongful denials for my son, our patients, students, and parents, effectively providing the solution for our children's success. We will dive deeply into the current understanding of autism discovered through our life's journey despite pharmaceutical, educational, familial, and criminal damage endured during the process. We will debunk flawed labels and practices, offering truthful justice for all those diagnosed with autism spectrum disorders. The latter portion includes sample reports that can serve as a tool in changing your autism-diagnosed loved one's life.

Quite simply, the $262 billion-dollar annual services cost solution is to implement all the chapters from Hope for Autism in our schools and treatment centers (Buescher, et al., 2014). Nearly 68 percent of our children will not participate in the labor force in their lifetime and this need to be justly corrected. (Bureau of Labor Statistics, 2014). We can, however, help the 2.4 million people with a co-morbid intellectual disability cost over their lifespan if we treat them medically rather than psychiatrically. We can remedy the flawed mindset that those with autism can't when we know they can.

CHAPTER 1

Autism: My Life, My Passion

How do we know precisely what constitutes 'normality' or mental illness? Conventional wisdom suggests that specially trained professionals have the ability to make reasonably accurate diagnoses. In this research, however, David Rosenhan provides evidence to challenge this assumption. What is—or is not—'normal' may have much to do with the labels that are applied to people in particular settings.

—DAVID L. ROSENHAN
"ON BEING SANE IN INSANE PLACES," 1973

In 2000, I was a 22-year-old, nine-months-pregnant mother starting graduate school when my beautiful first-born, Danielle, broke out in life-threatening hives after receiving her 12-month scheduled vaccinations. Her entire body was covered in rashes. She developed an extremely high fever and her face swelled to the point that breathing was difficult, requiring a trip to the emergency room. The doctors recommended Benadryl and rest. We were told she would be fine. Her father, a 22-year-old Los Angeles Police Department (LAPD) officer, and I thought nothing of it. She healed within a couple weeks and was our same little girl. She *seemed* fine.

At this exact time, my daughter exhibited what I now know was an epigenetic immune system response inherited through my

DNA to multiple vaccines given at one time. I realized this after a "hippietype" woman in our graduate program gave a lecture to more than 200 students on the complication of pharmaceuticals and government nepotism.

The lecture hall was full of eager graduate students hoping to become school counselors, school administrators, and marriage and family therapists with an applied behavioral analysis specialty. I listened intently, proud of myself for receiving a bachelor's degree in social work and having an insatiable heart for volunteering, helping, and teaching low-income Latino and black families in the inner cities of East and South-Central Los Angeles. I believed I was trying my best to heal myself, heal others, and stand up for liberty, justice, and freedom. The majority of us in that hall, however, trusted our government to protect our future generations. We all thought she was paranoid and delusional.

A year later, I was a 23-year-old mother of two beautiful children and finishing graduate school when my precious 15-month-old son, Dominic, developed a 105-degree fever, suffered febrile seizures, and became extremely ill after receiving his 12-month scheduled vaccinations. Rushing him to the ER, I was told again that sometimes children have this reaction to vaccines, but he would be fine. But he was not medically fine. He is still not medically fine. According to the compelling research on what causes these psychiatric labels of autism, ADHD, bipolar, etc., I am also not fine. The bottom line is trauma and injury to the brain, the gut, and other systems regulating the human body.

I watched in horror as my once vivacious, affectionate, playful, talkative son stopped looking at us and stopped sleeping. He screamed and clawed at me nonstop, refused to eat healthy food, pushed me away at the slightest touch, and started hand flapping. He was obsessed with small-part objects and puzzles, lost most of the motor skills he once had, and no longer played with his sister, Danielle, who he had utterly adored and called "Dada." Panicked and mortified, I kept taking him to the ER, to specialists, and to early-intervention government agencies, where no explanation or hope was offered. I argued with doctors, schools, and regional centers that this couldn't be autism or mental retardation based on the current scientific medical research about vaccines, vaccines with warning labels about viral encephalitis. I adamantly explained that the symptoms pointed to acquired viral encephalitis from the vaccine.

The conclusion was apparent: Like the lecturer at my graduate school, I was now the frowned-upon woman with paranoia and delusions who was pleading for help against dangerous vaccines, pharmaceutical companies, and an incompetent, corrupt government. Within months of my assertive appeals to doctors and government agencies alleging Dominic was sick from the vaccines, my son's condition was psychiatrically mislabeled "autism." No one would listen to me, even though I was highly educated and extremely professional.

I stopped sleeping well out of panic, cried often, started having nightmares, and had uncontrollable guilt-ridden flashbacks. I withdrew into the world of online research, read research articles and books, attended national Talk About Curing Autism (TACA) conferences, and tried countless experimental treatments to help my clearly sick son. I felt scared and alone, like my heart and soul had been ripped from me. I tried to stay as strong and hopeful as I could, loving him and his sister more than anything in this world.

Never giving up, I have spent his entire life advocating for truth, justice, and liberty against doctors, insurance companies, school districts, regional centers, social workers, teachers, police, and lawyers, but it was to no avail. I called it "Google syndrome." I was studying everything I could get my hands on—evidence based on experimental ideas, including Applied Behavior Analysis (ABA),

Pictures Exchange Communication System (PECS), biomedical therapies with Defeat Autism Now (DAN) methodologies, Rapid Prompting Method (RPM), Relationship Development Intervention (RDI), Neurofeedback, Biofeedback, Quantitative Electroencephalographs, Brain Gym, and many others.

Dominic was receiving unsuccessful treatments by doctors, schools, and regional centers that labeled him severely autistic and mentally retarded with no hope for the future. Denial after denial and poor services after poor services left us hopeless and angry. I would not give up or settle for such an obviously flawed diagnosis. My son, my students, and my patients were intelligent, resilient, and worthy of our investment. I started writing to program design schools, clinics, and tutoring centers to convey hope for all our vaccine-injured "autistic" children, while secretly trying to save my failing marriage.

I continued treating my son academically and therapeutically at home with the limited time I had, while also caring for his newly arrived siblings, Devin and Daliah, working full time, and obtaining hours toward my clinical license to practice psychotherapy. My son was making progress with me, with the limited time I had trying to be a wonderful, balanced mother for all my children, but he wasn't making any progress with others. When I would challenge his teachers or in-home providers about why they couldn't duplicate my success, they were immediately defensive, reminding me that he was severely retarded. In fact, I was retaliated against quite frequently with false child abuse complaints, slander, and defamation of character within my professional field. We were having break-ins at my home and my business; we were plagued with robbery and theft. It was depressing, frustrating, and exhausting. Dominic's dad at the LAPD simply checked out and become one of those who revolted against us utilizing gaslighting tactics.

The final straw was when Dominic began having life-threatening grand mal seizures, continually receiving false labels of autism and mental retardation, and receiving extreme mistreatment at his school. I would walk in unannounced to find him sleeping on floors, soiled, unfed, and covered with bruises, bite marks from other kids, and countless physical injuries from staff negligence. Enough was enough when the teacher called in a child abuse report of neglect and child endangerment against his dad and I when we confronted the school on its failure to provide an education commensurate with Dominic's Individualized Education Program (IEP). The truth was that I gave the government and inept, outdated treatment providers their shot for years, trusting they would do a good job with my son. What a joke. I knew then that I had to forever protect my son's future and protect his siblings from retaliation against the government that my tax dollars paid to supposedly care for them.

Thank God, my family had afforded me an inheritance, entrusted to me to carry on my fight for my son, my students, and my patients. They too had fought for humanity as NASA editors, Princeton attorneys, New York Times journalists, aviation pilots, helicopter pilots, and land developers. So, I quit work and put all my effort into finishing the development of my programs for Hope, Inc. I did this out of my home, providing my son with his education and psychotherapy treatments, including Applied Behavior Analysis, Rapid Prompting Method, RDI Floortime, Neurofeedback, Biofeedback, Applied Behavioral Analysis, Eye Movement Desensitization and Reprocessing, and Brain Gym at that time.

My son prospered, proving he was intelligent by making massive gains. He began to type independently with the special program I developed from watching how he learned. We also proved, sadly, that rather than suffering from a psychiatric diagnosis of autism, he suffered from an autoimmune disease caused by the viral encephalitis, which in turn damaged his stomach and various other systems.

Now I knew the truth about these newly made-up labels that were destructive for humanity: autism, attention deficit hyperactivity disorder (ADHD), obsessive-compulsive disorder (OCD), speech delay, depression, mental retardation (MR), and so on. And I knew how the mentally ill are treated in the United States, so I made a lifelong commitment to my children that I would never stop, no matter what anyone did to me or my children. If activists Erin Brockovich and Rosa Parks could make changes for the better in this world, I could too! Ironically, those have always been my nicknames: the Erin Brockovich of Autism and the Rosa Parks of special needs.

I brought back all I learned in order to treat and advocate for my children and Dominic's friends. Hope, Inc. grew exponentially, too quickly in fact, helping more and more sick children wrongfully denied by insurance companies, regional centers, and school districts in San Bernardino, Riverside, Orange, and Los Angeles counties. We offered the best of therapies, advocacy, and educational services for the mentally impaired I could learn along with Dominic.

The research I collected from patients, students, and families over two decades now comprises more than 700 accounts of how government and pharmaceutical industry corruption has led to a seriously flawed notion that our children and families are unworthy. I took the extreme measures of developing programs, testifying, settling more than $30 million dollars in compensation, and proving that the current definitions of autism and other disorders in the DSM must be revised.

As a mother and professional, I have donated every resource I have ever had, including sacrificing my own mind, body, and spirit to demonstrate transparency, accountability, and outcomes to the many who have failed to protect us along our mission. I survived cancer, in home invasions, domestic violence, life threatening car accidents, police brutality, attempted murders, fraud, thefts, retaliation, and doctors erroneously labeling me schizophrenic prescribing mind altering drugs causing drug induced psychosis. I have sacrificed my life, the safety of my children, my reputation, and the financial welfare of my family to achieve this mission for quality mental health and educational services that are ethical.

Against all odds, Dominic and I have discovered cutting-edge neuroscience and biomedical solutions. We would like to share our secrets with you, proving our children are not disabled but are brilliantly-abled. Access this link for helpful information for those in ABA-covered states on getting trained while providing services to their children: http://www.asha.org/Advocacy/state/States-Specific-Autism-Mandates/.

There is hope for autism.

CHAPTER 2

The Current, Flawed Definition of Autism

The current misnomer "autism" is defined as a group of brain-based developmental disabilities, characterized by impaired social communication and interaction, along with restricted, repetitive behaviors, interests, or activities. Those currently diagnosed with autism are diagnosed as such because they are eclectically diversified, lack eye movement, observably do not make eye contact or make little eye contact, do not seem interested in others, and do not show as much interest in people as they do in inanimate objects. Furthermore, there is often limited reaction to sounds, difficulties displaying a social smile, or watching others' faces when spoken to. The truth is, however, our children are uniquely brilliant, communicative, and social when perceived through the Hope for Autism lenses.

Their speech develops slowly, or not at all, with limited or no response to their own names or sounds. Other speech peculiarities include sometimes echoing what others are saying and displaying a somewhat robotic language. In addition, they do not try to engage others interactively, remain off topic, prefer to be alone with obsessions, engage in repetitive activities, cannot track where others are pointing to, or track objects that are moving. They do not point in order to show others their interests or needs, and they have limited engagement with interactive gestures of sharing. Empathy is lacking when others express emotion; there are struggles with greetings or departures, and they might not appear to be affectionate.

Moreover, they do not show a caring or concerned reaction to other people when they cry or appear to be in distress, have difficulty learning new routines or engaging in play, struggle with social language interaction, and do not learn simple interactive routines. The diagnosed child might lack affection and prefer to fixate on particular items. They might also display difficulty with change, repetitive hand flapping, spinning, tiptoe walking, unusual sleep patterns, and sensitivity to environmental visuals, noises, smells, and movements.

According to the Diagnostic Statistical Manual 5 (DSM 5), Autistic Spectrum Disorder 299.00 is characterized by the following criteria.

1. Persistent deficits in social communication and social interaction across multiple contexts, as manifested by the following, currently or by history (examples are illustrative, not exhaustive, see text):

    a. Deficits in social-emotional reciprocity, ranging, for example, from abnormal social approach and failure of normal back- and-forth conversation; to reduced sharing of interests, emotions, or affect; to failure to initiate or respond to social interactions.

    b. Deficits in non-verbal communicative behaviors used for social interaction, ranging, for example, from poorly integrated verbal and nonverbal communication; to abnormalities in eye contact and body language or deficits in understanding and use of gestures; to a total lack of facial expressions and nonverbal communication.

    c. Deficits in developing, maintaining, and understanding relationships, ranging, for example, from difficulties adjusting behavior to suit various social contexts; to difficulties in sharing imaginative play or in making friends; to absence of interest in peers.

2. Restricted, repetitive patterns of behavior, interests, or activities, as manifested by at least two of the following, currently or by history (examples are illustrative, not exhaustive; see text):

   a. Stereotyped or repetitive motor movements, use of objects, or speech (e.g., simple motor stereotypes, lining up toys or flipping objects, echolalia, idiosyncratic phrases).

   b. Insistence on sameness, inflexible adherence to routines, or ritualized patterns or verbal nonverbal behavior (e.g., extreme distress at small changes, difficulties with transitions, rigid thinking patterns, greeting rituals, need to take same route or eat food every day).

   c. Highly restricted, fixated interests that are abnormal in intensity or focus (e.g., strong attachment to or preoccupation with unusual objects, excessively circumscribed or perseverative interest).

   d. Hyper- or hypo-reactivity to sensory input or unusual interests in sensory aspects of the environment (e.g., apparent indifference to pain/temperature, adverse response to specific sounds or textures, excessive smelling or touching of objects, visual fascination with lights or movement).

3. Symptoms must be present in the early developmental period (but may not become fully manifest until social demands exceed limited capacities, or may be masked by learned strategies in later life).

4. Symptoms cause clinically significant impairment in social, occupational, or other important areas of current functioning.

5. These disturbances are not better explained by intellectual disability (intellectual developmental disorder) or global developmental delay. Intellectual disability and autism spectrum disorder frequently co-occur; to make comorbid diagnoses of autism spectrum disorder and intellectual disability, social communication should be below that expected for general developmental level.

Note: Individuals with a well-established DSM-IV diagnosis of autistic disorder, Asperger's disorder, or pervasive developmental disorder not otherwise specified should be given the diagnosis of autism spectrum disorder. Individuals who have marked deficits in social communication, but whose symptoms do not otherwise meet criteria for autism spectrum disorder, should be evaluated for social (pragmatic) communication disorder.

The following table from the DSM 5 determines severity levels for autism spectrum disorder.

Severity level	Social communication	Restricted, repetitive behaviors
Level 3 "Requiring very substantial support"	Severe deficits in verbal and nonverbal social communication skills cause severe impairments in functioning, very limited initiation of social interactions, and minimal response to social overtures from others. For example, a person with few words of intelligible speech who rarely initiates interaction and, when he or she does, makes unusual approaches to meet needs only and responds solely to very direct social approaches.	Inflexibility of behavior, extreme difficulty coping with change, or other restricted/ repetitive behaviors markedly interferes with functioning in all spheres. Great distress/difficulty changing focus or action.
Level 2 "Requiring substantial support"	Marked deficits in verbal and nonverbal social communication skills; social impairments apparent even with supports in place; limited initiation of social interactions; and reduced or abnormal responses to social overtures from others. For example, a person who speaks simple sentences, whose interaction is limited to narrow special interests, and who has markedly odd nonverbal communication.	Inflexibility of behavior, difficulty coping with change, or other restricted/repetitive behaviors appear frequently enough to be obvious to the casual observer and interfere with functioning in a variety of contexts. Distress and/or difficulty changing focus or action.
Level 1 "Requiring support"	Without supports in place, deficits in social communication cause noticeable impairments. Difficulty initiating social interactions, and clear examples of atypical or unsuccessful response to social overtures of others. May appear to have decreased interest in social interactions. For example, a person who is able to speak in full sentences and engages in communication but whose to-and-from conversation with others fails, and whose attempts to make friends are odd and typically unsuccessful.	Inflexibility of behavior causes significant interference with functioning in one or more contexts. Difficulty switching between activities. Problems of organization and planning hamper independence.

The DSM 5 adds a new diagnosis for Social (Pragmatic) Communication Disorder 315.39, which is characterized by the following criteria.

A. Persistent difficulties in the social use of verbal and nonverbal communication as manifested by all of the following:

1. Deficits in using communication for social purposes, such as greeting and sharing information, in a manner that is appropriate for the social context.

2. Impairment of the ability to change communication to match context or the needs of the listener, such as speaking differently in a classroom than on the playground, talking differently to a child than to an adult, and avoiding use of overly formal language.

3. Difficulties following rules for conversation and storytelling, such as taking turns in conversation, rephrasing when misunderstood, and knowing how to use verbal and nonverbal signals to regulate interaction.

4. Difficulties understanding what are not explicitly stated (e.g., making inferences) and nonliteral or ambiguous meanings of language (e.g., idioms, humor, metaphors, multiple meanings that depend on the context for interpretation).

B. The deficits result in functional limitations in effective communication, social participation, social relationships, academic achievement, or occupational performance, individually or in combination.

C. The onset of the symptoms is in the early developmental period (but deficits may not become fully manifest until social communication demands exceed limited capacities).

D. The symptoms are not attributable to another medical or neurological condition or to low abilities in the domains or word structure and grammar, and are not better explained by autism spectrum disorder, intellectual disability (intellectual developmental disorder), global developmental delay, or another mental disorder.

There are indisputable arguments raised by this current definition of autism (which is flawed) in light of advancement in neuroscience when alternate methods of communication, commonly referred to as augmentative and alternative communication (AAC), are employed. The symptoms of children with change drastically when their vastly ignored, core issues, of motor integration, processing, and sensory impairments are remedied. Their eye contact, daily living, and affection improves, their desire to socialize is evident, communication occurs in subsidized manners, empathy is observed, and their interests are absolutely expanded.

Diagnostic Assessment Procedures

There are a variety of assessment tools and interview formats utilized to diagnose children with autism. The most commonly used are as follows.

- Functional Analysis Screening Tool (FAST)
- Reinforcement Assessment for Individuals with Severe Disabilities (RAISD)
- Motivation Assessment Scale (MAS)
- Gilliam Autism Rating Scale (GARS)
- Gilliam Asperger's Disorder Scale (GADS)
- Autism Diagnostic Interview, Revised (ADI-R)
- Autism Diagnostics Observation Schedule (ADOS)
- Autism Spectrum Rating Scale (ASRS)

- Childhood Autism Rating Scale (CARS)
- Assessment of Basic Language and Learning Skills (ABLLS)
- Verbal Behavior Milestones Assessment and Placement Program (VB-MAPP)
- Conners Comprehensive Behavior Rating Scales (Conners CBRS)
- Vanderbilt Assessment Scale

Consumer assessment procedures, timelines, and instruments are used for diagnosis, including an explanation of how each instrument is applicable in assessing the consumer's needs. At Hope, Inc., we employ the ADOS, ADI-R, Conners CBRS, Vanderbilt, CARS, GADS, GARS, ASRS, and other neuropsychiatric testing inventories to determine a consumer's current level of functioning as a guide toward future success in our behavioral program.

Alternatively, Hope, Inc., uses ABLLS, developed by James W. Partington, PhD, BCBA, and Mark L. Sundberg, PhD, as a means of evaluating each consumer's behavioral deficits in the areas of visual performance, receptive language, imitation, vocal imitation, requesting behavior, labeling, conversation, play and leisure, social and group skills, academic skills, self-help skills, and motor skills. Once the necessary assessments are complete, an individual behavioral plan, infinite personal possibilities (IPP), and individual family service plan (IFSP) objectives are developed, based on the results of the inventories and observations. These assessments are performed in the two weeks of placement and are updated on a biannual basis. Utilization of assessment data for determining the specific activity and program services consumers receive is crucial.

Possible Screening Tools

Screening Tool	Authors	Screens	Who Completes	Format	Level
Checklist for Autism in Toddlers	Barren-Cohen, Allen, & Gillberg, 1992	18-month visit	Trained practitioner & parents	Structured interview, observation	1
Modified Checklist for Autism in Toddlers, Revised	Robins, Fein, & Barton, 2009	16–30 months	Trained practitioner & parents	Structured interview, observation	1
Screening Tool for Autism in Toddlers & Young Children	Stone, et al., 2000	24–36 months	Trained practitioner & parents	Structured interview, observation	2
Fill					

Assessment Tool	Authors	Edition	Severity	Who Completes	Format	Level
GARS—Gilliam Autism Rating Scale	Gilliam, 2003	3	3–22 years	Trained practitioner & parents	Structured interview form	1

Assessment Tool	Authors	Edition	Severity	Who Completes	Format	Level
GADS—Gilliam Asperger's Disorder Scale	Gilliam, 2013		3–22 years	Trained practitioner & parents	Structured interview form	1
ASRS—Autism Spectrum Rating Scales	Goldstein & Naglieri, 2009		2–18 years	Teachers, trained practitioner & parents	Structured Rating Scales	1

The vast spectrum of symptom variations we are witnessing from this epidemic calls for us to consider a new model of thinking about the true definition of "autism" and its diagnosis and treatment. When we treat people with individual medical and educational interventions based on medicine, they can and do improve.

Treating the viruses, bacteria, and toxins and improving the immune functioning of individuals labeled "autistic" shows that they do improve. We have the data to prove this. The brave doctors, clinicians, educators, attorneys, and others all have enough data compiled to prove that there is an autism correlation to neuroimmune injury. These children are smart, and they can be helped medically and educationally when viewed from this perspective.

Consider the following chart.

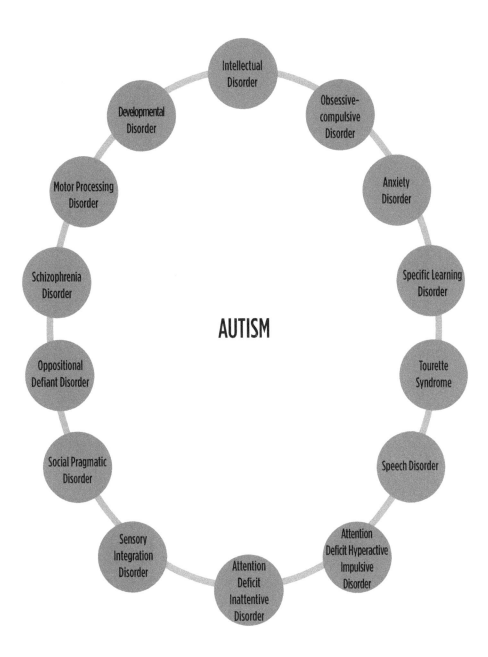

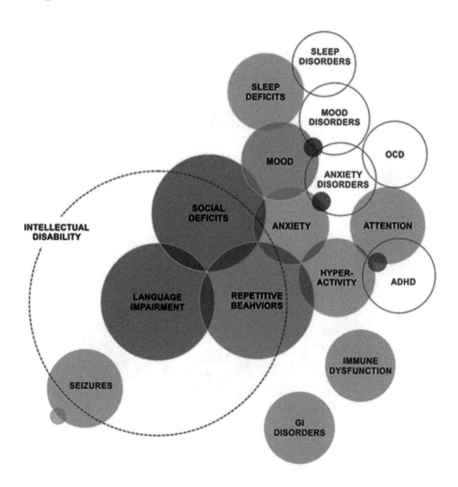

Psychiatrist Leo Kanner, considered the founder of autism, was simply wrong in my opinion. These children are physically sick due to a global preventable injury combined with genetic predisposition; they are smart but have different forms of social norms, communication, and intelligence. I watched my healthy, precious son deteriorate in front of me after a 105-degree fever and febrile seizures within hours of receiving six vaccines. Doctors said he would be fine. My son was not fine.

Dominic and I feel the same about so many of the labels in the DSM, which is in need of serious reform. Not that we don't need a manual or guide, but the who, the how, and the control of insurance companies, treatment providers, educators, and interventions is in serious need of reform. The manual should be simply brain- and body-based, not individually biased.

Most importantly, the emerging generations of autism, attention deficit hyperactivity disorder, and speech delay sufferers are worth our efforts to rehabilitate and educate humanely with social justice and programs that honor the Darwinist survival skills of these amazing children's resilient brains. The Diagnostic and Statistical Manual of Mental Disorders (DSM), published by the American Psychiatric Association, must be completely revised to reflect a new way of thinking about labeling and categorizing patients for diagnosis and treatment.

CHAPTER 3

The Autistic Brain and Immune System Connection

"My body feels like it is on fire, and I tell it to do something but it will not. Living in my body and having my mind feels like hell on earth, but I am strong and will do my best to change how the world views this new syndrome inaccurately labeled 'autism.' I don't have autism, Mom. I have an injury from those vaccines with brain scans and blood work to prove it. Why won't the medical and education systems listen to us? We could change the world, Mom."

—DOMINIC S. JUAREZ

Data compiled by the Centers for Disease Control and Prevention (CDC) confirms there is an indisputable, steep rise in the prevalence of autism spectrum disorder (ASD) in the United States over a relatively short period of time, which is uncorrelated to the theories on over reporting. We are currently at an alarming diagnosis rate of one in forty-five. It has already taken two decades of science to disprove the false theory of over reporting. We don't have another two decades to ignore the probable environmental triggers causing "autism" for those with predisposed genetic and epigenetic conditions.

There truly has been no unbiased, independent, ethical study completed ruling out all possible independent variables against dependent variables to determine if vaccine injury is causing these psychiatric impairments. How do we determine the ever-growing and changing impacts to our minds and bodies, such as vaccines, chemicals, food, water, air, etc., against predetermined DNA? The truth is that no one has EVER ruled out that vaccines don't cause autism. In fact, the US government acknowledges this injury with the National Vaccine Injury Compensation Program causing viral encephalitis.

The epidemiological, hypothetical basis for an immune system deficit correlated with neurological viral encephalitis and seizures is cited in several articles and medical journals, if one knows where to look. Theorized, this sharp rise can be attributed to a generational change of children inheriting predisposed autoimmune and neuroimmune conditions via Haemophilus Influenzae, Type B (HIB) and the combined measles, mumps, rubella (MMR) vaccine. Other studies suggest similar experiences about epidemiologic rates of ASD in Denmark and Israel, equally correlated with their country's introduction to HIB and Streptococcus Pneumoniae vaccines.

Dr. Kevin J. Tracey and The Feinstein Institute for Medical Research have undergone clinical trials to demonstrate how the vagus nerve plays a role in regulating inflammation. Scientists and doctors previously believed that the brain was completely separate from the body's other influences. However, this has been shown to be false.

The brain directly communicates with the immune system, which controls the body's response to infection and autoimmune disease. The vagus nerve plays a role in epilepsy, and according to Dr. Roberto Tuchman, a pediatric neurology specialist, and Michael Rosanoff, director of Autism Speaks, those with autism suffer from epilepsy at a rate of between 20 to 40 percent. Understanding how the brain, central nervous system, somatic nervous system, and vagus nerve all interact is key to understanding how a virus can derail the systems, causing major symptoms to be mislabeled as solely psychiatric autism.

Inflammation of the brain is known as encephalitis. Viral infections are the most common cause of this condition. Research from the Mayo Clinic also cites that encephalitis can occur in two ways, from direct infection of the brain or from a previous infection that causes the immune system to attack the brain. Johns Hopkins Bayview Medical Center notes that acute encephalitis is an inflammatory condition of the central nervous system. It is caused by a variety of conditions, including bacterial or viral infection of the brain, ingestion of toxic substances, complication of an infectious disease, and/or complication of an underlying malignancy.

Viruses such as encephalitis gain access to the central nervous system (CNS) through the blood or by traveling through nerve cells. The CNS consists of the brain and spinal cord. The peripheral nervous system is divided into the somatic nervous system and the autonomic nervous system. The somatic nervous system is associated with the voluntary control of body movements via skeletal muscles, whereas the autonomic nervous system controls involuntary systems, such as heart rate, digestion, and salivation. The vagus nerve is responsible for such varied tasks as heart rate, gastrointestinal peristalsis, sweating, and quite a few muscle movements in the mouth, including speech.

Symptoms of encephalitis include, but are not limited to, the following.

- Fever
- Headache
- Sensitivity to light or sound
- Confusion

- Poor memory/memory loss
- Loss of motor control
- Disorientation
- Hyperactivity
- Irritability
- Anxiety
- Seizures
- Weakness or numbness of arms or legs
- Fatigue

Dominic's current autism specialist is Dr. Jerry Kartzinel, who co-authored *Healing and Preventing Autism: A Complete Guide* with Jenny McCarthy. Jenny McCarthy is a role model to Mother Warriors and Trojans around the world. She stood up publicly first with Jim Carrey when others were too scared. Dr. Kartzinel has medical evidence of thousands of children like many of us, treating biological symptoms resulting from vaccine injury, whether the children were directly exposed or through epigenetic influences.

The National Vaccine Injury Fund acknowledges damage from viruses, toxins and bacteria. However, the moment our children are labeled with autism the cases are thrown out despite the medical evidence that this is exactly what "autism" is. For the rare families who don't vaccinate, but still have children with autism, it is important to remember that there are epigenetic precursers. We were vaccinated. We have autoimmune conditions. As 2017, the federal government has paid out more than $3.5 billion, but if public corruption was actually addressed, it would be in the trillions—trillions that are depleting our budgets.

Gut Problems
- Inflammatory bowel disease

- Reflux esophagitis
- Abnormal microbiome
- Leaky gut
- Malabsorption

Immunologic Problems
- Persistent viral/bacterial infection
- Food/environmental allergies
- Recurring illnesses
- Autoimmune
- Inflammation

Neurologic Problems
- Seizures/sensory issues
- Low muscle tone—especially trunk
- Perfusion defects—single photon emission-computed tomography (SPECT)
- Opiate effect

Metabolic/Detoxification Pathway Disruption
- Purine disorders
- Elevated ammonia
- Omega-3 fatty acid deficits
- Sulfation defect
- Methylation disorders
- Serotonin/melatonin deficit
- Dopamine defect
- Heavy metal burden

Vaccine Injury and Treatment Issues
for Dominic S. Juarez

Dr. Med. Gabriella Lesmo
Medico Specialista, FMH Pediatria , FMH Anestesiologia
Lugano Care Medical Center -Pian Scairolo 34 a - 6915
Lugano Noranco.
Tel. +41 (0) 91 993 21 10   Fax. +41 (0)91 993 21 32
Via IV Novembre 14 – 20019 Settimo Milanese
Cell. +39 339 162 6004
www.lesmoMD.com   E-mail: gabriella.lesmo@gmail.com

Biomedical Treatments for Children Development

Detoxification from environmental toxins, Mild HBOT, Metabolic rebalance
Sensory Learning Program®, Chelation, Craniosacral Therapy,

Autistic Syndromes, ADHD, Cerebral Palsy, Tourette's Disease, Developmental Delay
Learning Difficulties

To whom it may concern,

Dominic Juarez, born on 10.04.2000, is under my medical care for autism, epilepsy, sensory processing disorder, chronic fatigue, fibromyalgia and defects of both ankles that require the use of a wheelchair.

Dominic still has seizures, even if less frequent than some months ago.

Dominic is not verbal but he is able to communicate independently, typing on a keyboard and other communicators to key.

His metabolic disorder, frequently forced him to sleep 20 - 23 hours per day, with intermittent shower to ease his physical pain.

Due to his complex medication situation, Dominic needs to be placed on home hospital under Hope, Inc's care, to do intensive care with the aim to improve and to return to school in the future.

In order to preserve continuity of care, it would be in Dominic's best interest to continue to receive the care and services of Hope Inc. since they have a proven track record of being able to meet his needs.

If his parents conjointly agree to switch to a different team or company, they could consider the latter option, however, it should be stressed that Dominic should receive the same care from the same team at both parents' homes.

If you have any questions or concerns, please contact me at my office (gabriella.lesmo@lesmoMD.com).

Gabriella Maria Lesmo
07/16/2016

MD of Swiss Confederation GLN 7601000883254
Ordine dei Medici di Milano OMCEOMi. N. 19670
Albo dei Medici Omotissicologi OMCEOMi N. 62

Chromosomal Predisposition Issues

Dominic's previous autism specialist, Dr. Michael J. Goldberg, author of *The Myth of Autism: How a Misunderstood Epidemic Is Destroying Our Children*, deciphered similar conclusions, describing the crucial interactions among the brain, the vagus nerve, the gut, and the immune system, concluding the current definition is flawed and must be redefined. Neuroimmune Dysfunction Syndrome (NIDS) is an intended medical classification for illnesses or disorders (that might currently have psychiatric or developmental labels), which are caused by a complex neuroimmune, complex viral, autoimmune-like illness affecting cognitive and body functions in children and adults. Some of these diseases are labeled as autism, pervasive developmental disorder (PDD), attention deficit disorder (ADD) or ADHD, chronic fatigue syndrome/chronic fatigue immune dysfunction (CFS/CFIDS), as well as multiple related disorders. Many classic autoimmune diseases might have a treatable NIDS component.

In his early practice, Dr. Goldberg's wife developed what is now called CFS, a new and mysterious illness at the time also mislabeled as solely psychiatric. She was extremely ill, with physical symptoms, as well as debilitating cognitive effects, such as loss of short-term memory. When looking at her tests, Dr. Goldberg discovered markers that clearly indicated an immune/viral-based illness. Unfortunately, consultation with a variety of experts did not uncover any causes or suggest any treatments, but instead yielded the rather more stigmatizing assertion of a mental disorder.

Increasingly, Dr. Goldberg began to discover the presence of similar findings in children in his practice. These children came to him with the (formerly rare) label of "autism" or a new variant of ADHD. This added to the realization that these conditions were connected and furthermore had to be associated with a disease process. Functional magnetic resonance imaging (FMRI), SPECT scans, and quantitative electroencephalography (QEEG) continuously yielded damage commonly seen in the temporal and frontal lobe areas of the brain. This supports the claim that the observable spectrum of autism is a biological disease affecting various systems of the body and brain. Current research equally shows impacts to the muscular, cardiovascular, digestive, endocrine, nervous, and respiratory systems, and, most importantly, the immune lymphatic system.

These surprising observations led to a continuing search for causes, connections, and treatments for these diseases. By the late 1980s—through research, attending conferences and presentations, and consulting with experts in the fields of immunology and radiology— Dr. Goldberg realized that what he was seeing was a neuroimmune disease process. It was throwing off the brain, central nervous system, and the overall physical function in adult patients being discussed at conferences and in the children he was treating in his practice. Family histories of these children also revealed a high incidence of immune- mediated disorders, which correlated perfectly with his hypothesis.

Symptoms Found in NIDS

The symptoms of NIDS vary and can affect multiple areas of a child's development and overall health and well-being. The following symptoms might be present in a child with NIDS.

Cognitive
- Cognitive impairment
- Executive function impairment
- Headaches

- Inability to concentrate
- Irritability
- Lack of focus
- Obsessive-compulsive disorders
- Language delays

Neurological

- Abnormal EEGs or seizures
- Poor muscle tone
- Fine-motor and gross-motor abnormalities

Behavioral

- Inappropriate behaviors
- Poor socialization skills
- Poor eye contact

Whole body

- Fatigue
- Sallow color/complexion
- Poor growth and physical development

Allergy or illness expressions

- Low grade fevers
- Recurrent ear infections
- Multiple rashes
- Chronic congestion
- Multiple chemical and food sensitivities

- Dark circles under the eyes (usually viral but can sometimes be allergic/illness; red/reddish circles, commonly nicknamed "allergic shiners")
- Bright red cheeks

Gastrointestinal
- Bowel disturbances
- Irritable bowel syndrome (IBS)
- Colitis

Sensory
- Photosensitivity (a key disease indicator)
- Abnormal reactions to sensory input
- Auditory processing problems
- Vestibular processing problems

Sleep
- Sleep cycle or other sleep disturbances

Dr. Goldberg's NIDS protocol is only one viable and promising practice perspective among the many other brilliant approaches of caring doctors attempting to solve the autism puzzle. Practice perspectives include bacterial and toxin damage as well as viral injury from external sources. Interestingly, the aforementioned symptoms, when treated, often result in vast improvement.

There are many other notable doctors who would argue other promising practice perspectives on biological treatments that improve the functioning of autism. William Shaw, PhD, in Biological Treatments for Autism and PDD, states that the book includes information about therapies, such as the following.

- Secretin, CCK, and other GI hormones
- Gluten, casein, and soy sensitivity
- Vaccine reactions and vaccine recommendations
- Reversal of food allergies
- Transglutaminase antibody test for celiac disease
- Casein-free colostrum for immune deficiency
- NAET (allergy testing and allergy elimination treatment)
- Treatment and tests for mercury and other heavy metals
- DDP IV as the master regulator of peptide hormone metabolism
- Vancomycin reversal of autistic symptoms
- Amino acid abnormalities
- Diagnosis and treatment of causes of purine autism
- Calcium supplementation to prevent eye damage
- Bile salt deficiencies in autism
- Clostridia metabolite alteration of neurotransmitter metabolism
- Testing and treatment for succinylpurine autism

Another perspective about MMR, glyphosate, and autism is given by Dr. Stephanie Seneff, a senior MIT Research Scientist. She predicts that one in two children will be autistic by 2025. Dr. Andrew Wakefield, when he was a practicing gastroenterologist in Great Britain in the late 1990s, had a dozen or so children with gut dysbiosis (microbial imbalance) as patients who also suffered from significant developmental regression related to an encephalopathy condition. Many of these children seemed to show a pattern of significant deterioration following an MMR vaccine.

Together with several colleagues, in 1998 he published a case study in *The Lancet* on these children, which proposed that the live measles virus in the vaccine played a causal role in their condition, and that the disease process was related to unmetabolized proteins that escaped from the leaky gut and made their way into the brain, causing the encephalopathy. The ideas expressed in Wakefield's article should have been heralded as a major breakthrough in understanding the mechanism leading to autism, but instead, the article was retracted and he lost his license to practice medicine in Great Britain. Many believe that he was unfairly attacked due to the threat his article posed to the vaccine industry. The truth is we really do not know one way or the other. We do know many, many M.D.s argue for safer and more effective research when it comes to vaccines.

Gut issues have become prevalent among children today, with many children suffering from constipation and/or diarrhea, along with frequent abdominal pain. Allergic reactions to foods, such as gluten in wheat and casein in milk are often present in association with developmental delay and autism. "Leaky gut syndrome" has become a popular term to describe an inflammatory condition in the gut linked to leaky barrier function, which allows materials normally confined to the gut to distribute throughout the body. A leaky gut can induce a failure in the brain barrier as well, which then allows access to the brain for substances that are normally kept out.

A fascinating aspect of biology is the mechanism by which antibody responses to foreign proteins can induce autoimmune disease. The body's immune system has learned early in life to distinguish self from foreign proteins, but the distinction is graded, and sometimes foreign proteins can happen to resemble self-proteins sufficiently well that the immune cells get confused and attack the self-proteins as well as the foreign protein that it has committed to memory. This phenomenon is called "molecular mimicry," and it can occur following exposure to food sources of proteins, from a live infection, or from proteins introduced through vaccination.

With a leaky gut barrier, many more proteins get into the general circulation, such as undigested peptides from food sources, and the immune system then responds by memorizing these proteins and binding tightly to them to initiate a process that clears them from the circulation. A leaky brain barrier allows these foreign proteins access to the brain, and then there becomes a real threat of an autoimmune reaction to essential proteins in the brain, that happen to strongly resemble the foreign peptides through molecular mimicry.

One possibility to explain the increase in gut dysbiosis and food allergies observed today in industrialized countries is chronic exposure to a toxic chemical that is present in much of the food that children consume today. This chemical, called glyphosate, is the active ingredient in the pervasive herbicide, Roundup. Back when it was first introduced in the mid-1970s, glyphosate was heralded as a wonderful solution to the weed problem in agriculture, because it was claimed to be nearly nontoxic to humans.

In the mid-1990s, a new technology, involving "Roundup-Ready" crops, was approved, and then widely implemented in the United States. A bacterial gene inserted into the crop's DNA afforded it protection from glyphosate, which otherwise kills all plants. This technology was quickly adopted in corn, soy, canola, sugar beets, and alfalfa crops. Roundup could now be sprayed indiscriminately on the crop, and consequently, much more of the toxic chemical made its way into the food chain. Because the government believes that glyphosate is nearly nontoxic to humans, little monitoring is being done to assess the degree of exposure from food sources.

Glyphosate is a potent metal chelator, and it also has been patented as an antimicrobial agent. These two properties can easily contribute to a disruption of the balance between beneficial bacteria and pathogens in the gut. However, more ominously, glyphosate is a non-coding amino acid analog of glycine, the smallest amino acid. Amino acids are the building blocks of proteins, and glycine is often highly conserved in certain proteins that essentially depend on a glycine residue at that specific location in the protein chain in order to function properly. Recent research by research scientist Anthony Samsel and Stephanie Seneff shows strong evidence that glyphosate can substitute for glycine by mistake during protein synthesis. Not only would such a substitution often disrupt the protein's function in a profound way, but it would also make the protein resistant to being broken down.

How does this relate to the MMR vaccine? During the manufacturing process of the vaccine, the live measles virus is grown in a culture containing gelatin as a food source. The gelatin is derived from the ligaments of pigs that are fed mainly genetically modified glyphosate-resistant corn and soy feed. The main constituent of the gelatin is collagen, and collagen is a protein that contains a huge amount of glycine. This means that it is highly likely that the gelatin is contaminated with glyphosate.

The measles virus can then incorporate the glyphosate into its own proteins, in particular into a protein called hemagglutinin. Hemagglutinin is the key protein to which the human immune system responds by producing antibodies to it so that the measles virus will be immediately recognized and attacked, should it reappear at some future time. That is, the development of antibodies to hemagglutinin is what you are looking for to measure if the vaccination was successful in establishing immunity.

A series of seminal papers by Professor Ajay K. Singh and colleagues at Utah State University have shown that many children with autism have extremely high titers of antibodies to measles hemagglutinin. However, nearly all the children with the high antibody response also showed an autoantibody response to myelin basic protein. Myelin basic protein is an essential protein in the myelin sheath that surrounds major nerve fibers.

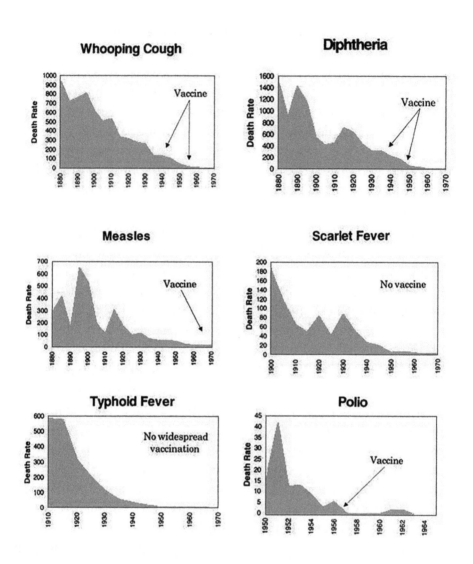

The live measles virus injected in the vaccine makes its way to the gut, where it settles in and flourishes, and then migrates from the gut to the brain, getting past the leaky gut barrier and leaky brain barrier that were induced by chronic glyphosate exposure in the food. Once the virus infects the brain, the brain's immune

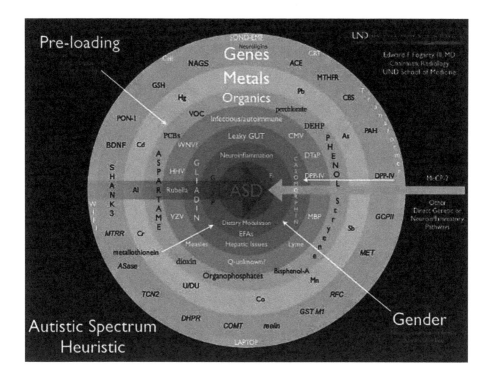

system develops antibodies to the virus hemagglutinin, which then, through molecular mimicry, also attacks the myelin sheath of the nerve fibers. This can destroy the ability of the fibers to carry out long-distance communications among widely separated neurons, which leads to the characteristic social and cognitive dysfunction of autism.

While the above scenario has not yet been proven conclusively, there is much evidence that supports it as a plausible theory for the epidemic we are seeing today in autism. The number of children with autism has been growing exponentially in the United States for the past three decades, in step with the exponential growth in the use of glyphosate-based herbicides on core crops. While correlation doesn't necessarily mean causation, the biological mechanisms outlined above by which glyphosate and MMR could collaborate to induce autism are highly suggestive of a causal link. Consider the following trends in the context of vaccines and the rates of disease declines.

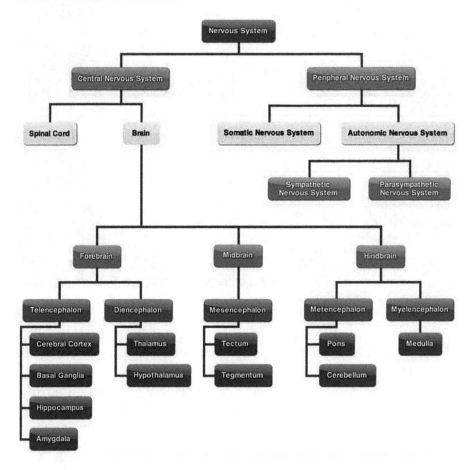

Considering the damage acknowledged by the CDC to cause vaccine injury, we are inaccurately labeling autism. Please review the Autism Spectrum Heuristic chart, developed by Dr. Edward F. Fogarty.

Our children are overwhelmingly medically ill from an environmental influence of viruses, bacteria, or toxins with a genetic predisposition that the mainstream has reported as psychiatric "autism," heavily focused on genetics rather than causes and treatments. Regardless of the nature-and-nurture argument continuing to exist in the science field of autism, wasting billions of dollars for argument's sake, one must simply and quickly put it in relational understanding with other commonly inherited viruses, toxins, and bacteria causing encephalitis to gain access to the central nervous system through blood or by traveling through nerve cells.

Here is an overview of the nervous system and its functions that might be impacted by the damage done to the brain, which results in what we are behaviorally and educationally observing.

The central nervous system consists of the brain and the spinal cord. The peripheral nervous system is divided into the somatic nervous system and the autonomic nervous system.

The somatic nervous system is associated with the voluntary control of body movements via skeletal muscles. The autonomic nervous system controls involuntary systems, such as heart rate, digestion, salivation, etc.

The vagus nerve is responsible for such varied tasks as heart rate, gastrointestinal peristalsis, sweating, and quite a few muscle movements in the mouth, including speech. It is quite relevant to all the seizures we are seeing: staring-off petite mals, grand mals, complex seizures, etc. Medical marijuana may be a solution according to many researchers compiling evidence. For example, Edward Maa, Chief of the Comprehensive Epilepsy Program at Denver Health and Hospitals, has done cutting edge research.

Cannabis sativa has a long history of medicinal use, with the earliest documentation around 4000 B.C. in China, for the treatment of rheumatism, pain, and convulsions. In fact, cannabis was available over the counter in U.S. pharmacies for a variety of maladies until 1941, following passage of the Marijuana Tax Act of 1937, which limited its access. Finally, the Controlled Substances

Act of 1970 classified cannabis as Schedule I, making its use illegal. Although the political environment surrounding "pot" hindered prospective human clinical investigation, researchers continued to elucidate the structure and activity of C. sativa. Mechoulam et al. determined the structure of Δ9-tetrahydrocannabinol (THC) and cannabidiol (CBD) in 1963. A few case reports suggested anticonvulsant activity associated with Δ9-THC, but psychotropic side effects were often rate limiting. A conflicting report suggested that the smoking of marijuana may be proconvulsant. In 1973, Carlini first demonstrated the anticonvulsant effects of CBD, noting the absence of any clear toxicity, and its lack of psychotropic effects. In 1975, Juhn Wada protected cats from kindled seizures with Δ9-THC, and prevented seizures in already kindled baboons. In 1980, Cunha et al. performed a randomized, double-blind, placebo controlled trial of 15 patients who received either CBD or a placebo in addition to their existing medication. Four of the eight patients "remained almost free" of convulsions; three additional patients demonstrated "partial improvement," and one of eight had no effect at all. In contrast, only one of the placebo patients showed improvement.

Part of the challenge of understanding why cannabis has apparently contradictory effects in epilepsy likely has to do with the complexity of the plant itself. Cannabis sativa has 489 known constituents, only 70 of which are cannabinoids, with the remainder including potentially neuroactive substances such as terpenes, hydrocarbons, ketones, aldehydes, and other small hydrophobic compounds capable of crossing the blood–brain barrier. The variability of the strain-specific ratios of the most common cannabinoid, Δx-THC, and the second most common cannabinoid, CBDx, offers further complexity in utilizing whole cannabis as an antiepileptic. In addition, the mode of administration likely affects bioavailability and neuroactivity. For instance, smoked and vaporized cannabis requires heat, which may alter the putative antiepileptic substance(s), whereas ingested cannabis must survive the acidic environment of the stomach and first pass through the metabolic system. The extraction method is also critical, as the conditions and solvents used to separate these phytocompounds may alter them in the process.

The attractiveness of isolating a single compound that is responsible for a specific desired attribute is not lost on physicians, patients, parents, growers, and scientists, but it is as likely that a combination of neuroactive substances taken together rather than a single substance is responsible for any potential antiepileptic effect. For instance, the endocannabinoid system was discovered when the endogenous receptor for Δ9-THC was identified in 1990. The seven transmembrane G protein–coupled receptor called cannabinoid receptor type 1 (CB1) mediates neuronal inhibition by promoting decreased calcium influx and increased potassium efflux. In 1992, the endogenous ligands to CB1 were identified: "anandamide," an arachidonic acid derivative, and 2-arachidonoyl glycerol (2-AG), a phosphatidyl inositol precursor. These endocannabinoids are produced on demand during excessive neuronal excitation and are felt to be part of a natural dampening feedback loop. However, they have been found on both γ-aminobutyric acid (GABA)ergic as well as glutamatergic neurons, so their net effect is not entirely predictable. Although this may offer one possible mechanism by which cannabis controls seizures (or exacerbates them), cannabidiol does not bind to CB1, and at this time its molecular target is not completely understood. CBD may be an agonist of 5-HT1a receptor, with similar affinity as serotonin, or an agonist of a novel endocannabinoid receptor GPR55. It is possible that CBD and Δ9-THC work synergistically to suppress seizures. In fact, Ethan Russo, senior medical advisor to GW Pharma, recently reviewed the evidence for the "entourage effect" of the phytocannabinoids and terpenoids, and he makes a strong case for their synergistic effects in a variety of disease states.

Based on conversations with the parents who are currently pursuing Charlotte's Web, the most compelling arguments for the need to study whole cannabis therapy are the concept of autonomy and availability. A naturally occurring and potentially effective herbaceutical is very attractive to these families. Apart from the daily challenges and emotional toll of caring for children with a high frequency of convulsions and/or drop attacks, the risk of sudden unexplained death in epilepsy (SUDEP) looms over these caretakers. The present availability of a potentially useful therapy is driving a flurry of families to uproot and relocate to Colorado. Although the excitement surrounding Epidiolex (GW Pharma's pharmaceutical grade CBD plant extract) is high among these families, their access to the clinical trial sites seem even more remote than trying their luck in Colorado, and many are not willing to wait the countless years of pharmaceutical approval anticipated for Epidiolex, as their children's SUDEP risk continues to accumulate. The obvious and very serious problem is that patients and families may mistake what available science there is behind cannabis research and attempt to extract whole plant compounds on their own. Anecdotal accounts have surfaced locally since the story of Charlotte aired on CNN of severe pediatric intoxications resulting from stovetop extractions with butter. Other reports reveal that in the haste of moving these children, proper transition planning is ignored and many are ending up in the intensive care unit in status epilepticus after their cross-country move. Also new since the airing of Charlotte's story, Colorado dispensaries are touting their own versions of "high CBD content" tinctures, ingestibles, and capsules. With little to no ability to keep up with the regulatory demands of the medical/recreational cannabis industry, quality control of available cannabis products is next to impossible at this time but critically needed.

Despite all of the challenges of medical marijuana as a potential therapy for epilepsy, what is not controversial is the need for a call for calm, and at the same time a call for thoughtful and thorough pharmacologic and clinical investigation into cannabis and its many constituent compounds to confirm or disprove its safety and antiepileptic potential. Growers and regulators must satisfy concerns about consistency, quality, and safety before medical cannabis will ever gain legitimacy as a mainstream therapeutic option. Investigations involving children with catastrophic epilepsy syndromes require well-conceived double-blinded placebo protocols. Not only are many of these children "at the end of the road" of therapeutic options, but some families have invested heavily to move to states with legalized cannabis, and the intense desire for a successful therapy can impact clinical trial results.

As would be expected, well-intentioned and well-informed physicians, lawmakers, patients, and parents come down on different sides of the cannabis question, but in states that have chosen to legalize cannabis, failure to understand the intense desire of a large population of patients with epilepsy to use medical cannabis for the treatment of epilepsy is foolish at best and dangerous at worst. In Colorado, we are at "ground zero" for this debate, and it behooves us to educate the public, quiet the frenzy, and inform the proper design and execution of clinical research that will answer the question of whether high concentration CBD cannabis is an effective antiepileptic agent.

Understanding further how the brain, central nervous system, somatic nervous system, and vagus nerve all interact is key to understanding how a virus can derail the systems causing major symptoms. To better this concept, look at how the brain is organized in these next images.

Parts of the Human Brain

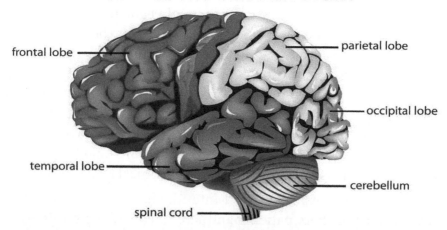

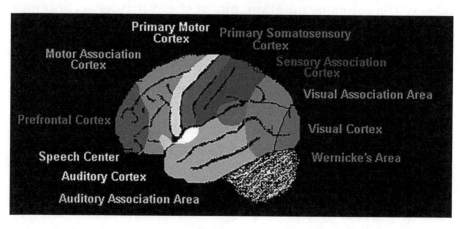

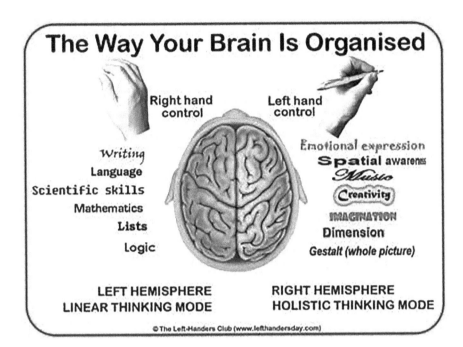

The Way Your Brain Is Organised

Right hand control

Left hand control

Writing
Language
Scientific skills
Mathematics
Lists
Logic

Emotional expression
Spatial awareness
Music
Creativity
IMAGINATION
Dimension
Gestalt (whole picture)

LEFT HEMISPHERE
LINEAR THINKING MODE

RIGHT HEMISPHERE
HOLISTIC THINKING MODE

© The Left-Handers Club (www.lefthandersday.com)

CHAPTER 4

The Autistic Brain, Behavior, and Learning Connection

"Efforts and courage are not enough without purpose and direction."

— JOHN F. KENNEDY

Dr. Leo Kanner, the "founder of autism," initially stated that autism was biological before changing his stance in 1949 that it was a psychiatric impairment. It is believed by some that his change in opinion came with the introduction of the diagnostic statistical manual, which was developed by a group of psychiatrists. His error in choosing psychiatry, a narrow-minded discipline, is precisely where the mislabeling of autism as psychiatric occurred. It derailed any progress that one diagnosed with autism would make with doctors. Unfortunately, they were biologically and physiologically treating what was clearly a disease or traumatic brain injury from a virus, toxins, or bacteria. Accordingly, the focus on causal environmental influences and biological treatments with genetic markers would have disproved Dr. Kanner's erroneous conclusions.

53

Had Dr. Kanner stayed effectively on the accurate mindset of a biological   illness comparative to lupus, cancer, Lyme disease, candidiasis, and others, the scientific and the educational domains would have focused on the functional brain and body interconnectivity for more precise, progressive medications, natureceuticals, therapies, educational services, and dietary management treatment methods. As priorities to rectify behaviors based on the brain, these would be much more impactful than solely a behavior management program as the primary intervention, which is common practice today.

It is helpful to understand the brain in terms of behavior and learning styles by first examining the brain's functions, structures, and interconnectivity of the lobes, cortical areas, and hemispheres. This translation helps in conceptualizing the current treatments, interventions, and educational methodologies, equally substantiating the current definition of autism and autism's symptoms, which are better accounted for by other disorders and diseases. Redefining autism according to what the brain translates into behavior, most notably visual, auditory, and motor processing impacts, is so powerful for designing new medication/natureceutical, therapeutic, educational, and dietary management treatment methods.

Brain Part	Function
Frontal Lobe	Creative thought, problem solving, intellect, judgment, behavior, attention, abstract thinking, physical reactions, muscle movement, coordinated movements, smell, and personality
Parietal Lobe	Comprehension, visual functions, language, reading, internal stimuli, tactile sensation, and sensory comprehension.
Temporal Lobe	Visual and auditory memories, helps manage some speech and hearing capabilities, behavioral elements, and language

Occipital Lobe	Helps control vision
Cerebellum	Commonly referred to as the "little brain," controls essential body functions such as balance, posture, and coordination, allowing humans to move properly and maintain their structure.

Cortical Area	Function
Prefrontal Cortex	Problem solving, emotion, complex thought
Motor Association Cortex	Coordination of complex movement sensory stimulation
Primary Motor Cortex	Initiation of voluntary movement
Primary Somatosensory Cortex	Receives tactile information from the body
Sensory Association Area	Processing of multisensory information
Visual Association Area	Complex processing of visual information
Visual Cortex	Detection of simple visual stimuli
Wernicke's Area	Language comprehension
Auditory Association Area	Complex processing of auditory information
Auditory Cortex	Detection of sound quality (loudness, tone)
Broca's Area	Speech production and articulation

Sensations	Over responsive "Oh no!"	Under responsive "Ho, hum"	Sensory-Seeking "More!"
Touch	Avoids touching Being touched	Unaware of contact with objects & body	Surrounding, touching, chewing
Movement / Balance	Avoids moving or being moved	Doesn't notice when moved; lacks initiation	Craves fast constant movement; spinning
Position & Muscle Control	Uncoordinated Rigid; Avoids certain play	Lacks inner drives; alertness increases after exertion	Craves being squeezed, seeks heavy work
Sights	Overexcited with too much work	Ignores new visual stimulation	Seeks visually stimulating scenes
Sounds	Covers ears to close out sound	Ignores ordinary sounds	Loves loud noises; crowds, TV, etc
Smells	Objects to odors others don't	Unaware of pleasant odors, smell of food	Seeks strong odors; others avoid
Tastes	Objects to textures & temperatures	May eat very spicy food; no reactions	May taste inedible items; like spicy food

Visual Motor Integration

Visual processing deficits, treated appropriately, can make a huge difference in understanding the new autism definition I propose from a neuroscience perspective. Vision is much more than accurate far and near eyesight from a brain-based perspective. The occipital lobes allow for decoding of symbols, pictures, distance, and integration of the physical body's awareness. Brain dysfunctions such as these are called visual processing disorders.

For example, the visual motor integration (VMI) consists of coordinating visual perceptual skills organized with gross-motor and fine-motor movements. Integrating visual input with motor output goes hand and hand. This is how we plan, execute, and monitor gross-motor and fine-motor tasks. The integration of the two is also essential in academic performance, social skills, communication, typing, emotional regulation, and self-esteem.

Eight Types of Visual Processing Issues to Consider

Visual processing issues are multifaceted. Many visual processing issues often go undetected. The following are the various types of visual processing issues identified in the medical community.

Visual discrimination issues: Children have difficulty distinguishing between two similar letters, shapes, or objects. Mixing up letters, confusing d and b and confusing p and q is common.

Visual figure-ground discrimination issues: Children with this type might not be able to pull out a shape or character from the background. Furthermore, they might have trouble locating specific information on a page, with the task often becoming difficult and overwhelming.

Visual sequencing issues: Children with these issues have difficulty telling the order of symbols, words, or images. Skipping lines when reading, and reversing or misreading letters, numbers, and words is commonplace. They might struggle with writing answers on a separate sheet of paper.

Visual motor processing issues: Children have trouble using feedback from the eyes to coordinate the movement of other parts of the body. Writing within the lines, not bumping into things, copying from a book, and typing are skills that are lacking.

Long-term or short-term visual memory issues: Children might have difficulty recalling what they have seen from long-term or short-term math, reading, and spelling prompts. Typing is a complicated task.

Visual spatial issues: Locating where objects are in space is problematic. Judging distance to an object is complicated, as well as comprehending time, maps, and characters described on paper or in a spoken narrative.

Visual closure issues: Identification of an object, or facial features when only certain parts are visible, is impacted. Spelling or word identification is also impacted due to letters or words vanishing in a narrative structure.

Letter and symbol reversal issues: Switching letters or numbers when writing is common. Letter formation is affected when reading, writing, and performing mathematical tasks.

The Right Brain vs. Left Brain

Damage commonly seen in QEEG, FMRI, and SPECT scans to the temporal and frontal lobe areas of the brain define the observable spectrum of autism. Theories exist about brain dominance and how it plays a role in thinking and behaving. The theory of left-brain or right-brain dominance, with each side of the brain controlling different types of thinking, suggests each side plays an integral role.

Additionally, people are said to prefer one type of thinking to the other. For example, a person who is "left-brained" is often said to be more logical, analytical, and objective, while a person who is "right-brained" is said to be more intuitive, thoughtful, and subjective. Theories also exist that suggest those with autism tend to use more of their right brain, with anomalies heavily affecting the left.

If one were to split the brain right down the middle into two symmetrical, or equal, parts, one would have a right and a left hemisphere. Although equal in size, these two sides are not the same and do not carry out the same functions. The left side of the brain is responsible for controlling the right side of the body. It also performs tasks that have to do with logic, such as in science and mathematics. On the other hand, the right hemisphere coordinates the left side of the body and performs tasks that have to do with creativity and the arts. Both hemispheres are connected by the corpus callosum and serve the body in different ways.

According to the left-brain, right-brain dominance theory, the right side of the brain is best at expressive and creative tasks. Some of the abilities that are popularly associated with the right side of the brain include facial recognition, emotional expressions, musical abilities, empathy, color, images, intuition, creativity, etc. The left side of the brain is considered to be skillful at logic, expressive language, mathematical, analytical thinking, reasoning, etc.

The corpus callosum, which separates the hemispheres, is also said to be heavily impacted for those with autism. A brain-based impairment, agenesis of the corpus callosum (ACC), is said to have extremely high co-morbid rates explaining the behavioral differences among the autism spectrum disorders. Most important, this explains the high rates of individualized sensory motor impairments also observed in autism.

Sensory Input Received from the Peripheral System: Current research indicates extreme sensory integration deficits and impedances for those with autism, but, ironically, limited research indicates benefits from sensory integration treatments. Perhaps one can view this as analogous to a human being inarguably ambulatory, and yet no treatments exist to cure ambulation. Professor Stephen Hawking's lips do not move, nor can he walk, after he contracted a motor neuron disease, but it is clearly evident that he possesses a brilliant mind. Tito, diagnosed with autism, cannot speak, walks with a poor gait, and performs hand flapping, yet, he is a brilliant poet.

Maintaining balance with a viral, bacterial, or toxin injury (labeled autism), varies, depending on the way the information received by the brain from the peripheral sources of the eyes, muscles, joints, and vestibular organs is integrated. These sources send information to the brain in the form of nerve impulses from special nerve endings called sensory receptors, which are often found to be damaged in those with autism.

Sensory receptors in the retina of the eye are called rods and cones. Light striking the rods and cones send impulses to the brain, providing visual cues, identifying how one feels oriented relative to other objects. For example, some children with autism walking along the street have difficulty identifying their surrounding orientation within their peripheral vision range. Most importantly, in education and behavioral interventions, their visual motor integration affects their ability to express what they consciously and cognitively know. This feeds the myth that the children are mentally retarded or incapable of immense progress.

The neck and ankle's sensory impulses are particularly important. Proprioceptive signals from the neck indicate the direction in which the head is to be turned, influencing what appears like a lack of focus and attention. Indications from the ankles designate the body's movement or control relative to both the upright surface floor and the information to the body's feedback, feeling hard, soft, slippery, or uneven. This can also be evidenced by awkward body movements, poor sports skills, and limited affection.

The skin, muscles, and joints involve sensory receptors that are sensitive to stretches or pressures derived from the proprioceptive information received in the surrounding tissues. For example, children with autism who receive increased pressure might tiptoe walk or even display intensified head banging as a result. Sensory receptors respond with brain impulses being sent with any movement of the legs, arms, and other body parts. This is why swinging, jumping, hand flapping, etc., might assist the tissues, but also why touch is uncomfortable to their bodies. It does not mean they don't desire touch, but rather, they simply can't tolerate the feelings associated with touch.

Motion, equilibrium, and spatial orientation information within the sensory systems is provided by the vestibular apparatus including the utricle, saccule, and three semicircular canals of the ear. Vertical gravity and linear movement is detected by the utricle and saccule, and rotational movement is detected by the semicircular canals when functioning accurately. The receptors send impulses to the brain about movement from the opposite sides of the brain, similar to hand dominances.

Sensory Integration Input: The brain stem receives balance information provided by the previously discussed peripheral sensory organs. The coordinator of the brain, the cerebellum, along with the thinking and memory hubs, and the cerebral cortex, are all either sorted and integrated or become discombobulated. Practiced automatic, learned movements from certain motions a person is exposed to become solidified in the cerebellum. However, oftentimes, they are impacted by the accurate definition of autism. This is why many children with mild to severe autism suffer from a lack of balance control during fine- and gross-motor movement tasks. Influences from the cerebral cortex include formerly learned material, but if prior information is not learned due to damage injury or failure to thrive, erroneous notions of limited intellect occur.

Sensory Processing Input Conflicts: The disorientated nature of autism is clearly an indication of conflicts within the peripheral systems. For example, feeling like one is moving when large objects pass before one's visual field, or seeing an item as two-dimensional (2D) when it is truly three-dimensional (3D). Sensory information provided by the vestibular organs might supersede this sensory clash, however, it often fails to occur in what we mislabel autism. We know this because these conflicts occur in other equally related autoimmune and degenerative conditions. Those with autism who appear extremely impacted with sensory issues report their higher-level thinking and memory attempts to remind the body, however, a disconnect often occurs as the poorly trained eye simply does not know where to look.

Motor Output: The brain stem transmits impulses to the muscles that control movements of the eyes, head, neck, trunk, and legs, allowing a person to both maintain balance and have a clear vision while moving when sensory integration actually occurs. A baby learns to balance through repetition sent from the sensory receptors to the brain stem, and then out to the muscles to form a novel pathway through facilitation. Yet, frequently we don't see this occurring in those with autism. Solid evidence exists suggesting that such synaptic reorganization occurs throughout a typical person's lifetime of adjusting to changing environments or health conditions, but oftentimes, with autism, we simply don't see this evolutionary transformation.

The vestibular system directs motor control signals through the nervous system to the muscles of the eyes with an involuntary role called the vestibule-ocular reflex. When the head is not moving, the number of impulses from the vestibular organs on the right side is equivalent to the number of impulses coming from the left side. The variance in impulses directed from separate sides controls eye movements and steadies the gaze during active head movements and passive head movements in the typically developing child. However, once again, this is often unregulated in those labeled autistic.

A Balanced Coordination System: Complex sets of sensorimotor-control systems define the human balance system. This is true particularly for those who are medically ill, while erroneously labeled psychiatrically impaired with autism. The interlocking feedback mechanisms needed for coordination are often disrupted by damage to one or more components through a virus, toxins, and bacteria from a combination of genetic predispositions paired with environmental exposures.

The complexity of the human balance system creates major challenges in diagnosing and treating the underlying cause of imbalance accurately when it comes to an autism diagnosis, especially with so much contradictory research. The vestibular system's interaction with perceived cognitive functioning, and the degree of influence it has on the control of eye movements and posture as a result of a vestibular dysfunction solves the intricate challenges to the flawed definition of autism.

If we simply see our children as medical impairments, we solve the puzzle and move forward in more accurate and progressive treatments in all domains of medicine, education, and therapy. To understand the totality of sensory and balance impedances for those misdiagnosed with a psychiatric impairment, such as "autism," author and music, movement, and drama teacher Carol Stock Kranowitz's chart succinctly organizes such complex subjects for a layperson's understanding.

Understanding the complex workings of the brain leads to a better understanding of behavior and how to make an accurate, workable diagnosis and treatment plan. The following chart likewise helps as a guide to seeing what strengths and weakness interventions should be targeted to assist in developmental progression using RPT, AAC, and RPM beneficially.

THE 7 STYLES **OF LEARNING**

VISUAL (SPATIAL):
You prefer using pictures, images, and spatial understanding.

- Use images, pictures, color and other visual media to help you learn
- Use color, layout, and spatial organization in your associations, and use many 'visual words' in your assertions.
- Use mind maps
- Replace words with pictures, and use color to highlight major and minor links

SOLITARY (INTRAPERSONAL):
You prefer to work alone and use self-study.

- You prefer to learn alone using self-study
- Align your goals and objectives with personal beliefs and values
- Create a personal interest in your topics
- When you associate and visualize, highlight what you would be thinking and feeling at the time
- You drive yourself by the way you see yourself internally
- Modeling is a powerful technique for you
- Be creative with role-playing
- Your thoughts have a large influence on your performance and often safety

AURAL (AUDITORY-MUSICAL):
You prefer using sound and music.

- Use sound, rhyme, and music in your learning
- Use sound recordings to provide a background and help you get into visualizations
- When creating mnemonics or acrostics, make the most of rhythm and rhyme, or set them to a jingle or part of a song
- If you have some particular music or song that makes you want to 'take on the world,' play it back and anchor your emotions and state.

SOCIAL (INTERPERSONAL):
You prefer to learn in groups or with other people.

- Aim to work with others as much as possible
- Role-playing is a technique that works well with others, whether its one on one or with a group of people
- Work on some of your associations and visualizations with other people
- Try sharing your key assertions with others
- Working in groups to practice behaviors or procedures help you understand how to deal with variations

VERBAL (LINGUISTIC):
You prefer using words, both in speech and writing.

- Try the techniques that involve speaking and writing
- Make the most of the word-based techniques such as assertions and scripting
- Record your scripts using a tape or digital audio recorder (such as an MP3 player), and use it later for reviews
- When you read content aloud, make it dramatic and varied
- Try working with others and using role-playing to learn verbal exchanges such as negotiations, sales or radio calls

PHYSICAL (KINESTHETIC)
You prefer using your body, hands and sense of touch.

- Focus on the sensations you would expect in each scenario
- For assertions and scripting, describe the physical feelings of your actions.
- Use physical objects as much as possible
- Keep in mind as well that writing and drawing diagrams are physical activities
- Use role-playing, either singularly or with someone else, to practice skills and behaviors

LOGICAL (MATHEMATICAL)
You prefer using logic, reasoning and systems.

- Aim to understand the reasons behind your content and skills
- Create and use lists by extracting key points from your material
- Remember association often works well when it is illogical and irrational
- Highlight your ability to pick up systems and procedures easily
- Systems thinking helps you understand the bigger picture
- You may find it challenging to change existing behaviors or habits
- If you often focus from analysis paralysis, write 'Do It Now' in big letters on some signs or post-it notes

bluemango
LEARNING SYSTEMS
www.bluemangolearning.com

Sources:
http://www.learning-styles-online.com/overview/

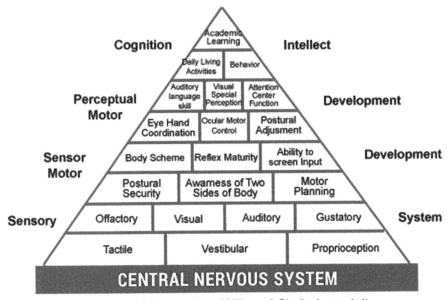

Pyramid of Learning. (Williams & Shellenbeger, 1-4)

CHAPTER 5

Empirically Supported Treatments and Promising Practices

"The best way to predict the future is to create it."

— PETER DRUCKER

Antecedent Package

These interventions involve the modification of situational events that typically precede the occurrence of a target behavior. These alterations are made to increase the likelihood of success or reduce the likelihood of problems occurring. Treatments falling into this category reflect research representing the fields of applied behavior analysis (ABA), behavioral psychology, and positive behavior supports.

Examples include, but are not restricted to, the following.

- Antecedent package
- Behavioral package
- Cognitive behavioral intervention
- Comprehensive behavioral treatment for young children

- Differential reinforcement
- Discrete trial teaching
- Exercise
- Extinction
- Functional behavior assessment
- Functional communication training
- Joint attention intervention
- Modeling
- Naturalistic teaching strategies
- Parent-implemented intervention
- Peer training package
- Picture exchange communication system
- Pivotal response treatment
- Prompting
- Reinforcement
- Response interruption / redirection
- Schedules
- Scripting
- Self-management
- Social narratives
- Social skills training
- Story-based intervention package
- Structured playgroups
- Task analysis
- Technology-aided instruction and intervention
- Time delay
- Video modeling
- Visual supports

Behavioral Package

These interventions are designed to reduce problem behavior and teach functional alternative behaviors or skills through the application of basic principles of behavior change. Treatments falling into this category reflect research representing the fields of ABA, behavioral psychology, and positive behavior supports.

Examples include, but are not restricted to, the following:

- Behavioral sleep package
- Behavioral toilet training/dry bed training
- Chaining
- Contingency contracting
- Contingency mapping
- Delayed contingencies
- Differential reinforcement strategies
- Discrete trial teaching
- Functional communication training
- Generalization training
- Mand training
- Noncontingent escape with instructional fading
- Progressive relaxation
- Reinforcement
- Scheduled awakenings
- Shaping
- Stimulus
- Stimulus pairing with reinforcement
- Successive approximation
- Task analysis
- Token economy

Behavioral Package: Treatments

Treatments involving a complex combination of behavioral procedures that might be listed elsewhere in this document are also included in the behavioral package category.

Examples include, but are not restricted to, the following.

- Choice + embedding + functional communication training + reinforcement
- Modeling + contingency management
- Non-contingent reinforcement + differential reinforcement
- Schedules + reinforcement + redirection + response prevention
- Task interspersal with differential reinforcement
- Tokens + reinforcement + choice + contingent exercise + overcorrection

Studies targeting verbal operants also fall into this category.

Cognitive Behavioral Intervention

Refers to a number of different but related interventions used to change behavior by teaching individuals to understand and modify thoughts and behaviors.

Comprehensive Behavioral Treatment for Young Children

This treatment reflects research from comprehensive treatment programs that involves a combination of applied behavior analytic procedures (for example, discrete trial, incidental teaching), which are delivered to young children (generally under the age of eight).

These treatments might be delivered in a variety of settings (home, self-contained classroom, inclusive classroom, community) and involve a low student-to-teacher ratio (for example, 1:1).

All the studies falling into this category meet the strict criteria of:

1. (a) targeting the defining symptoms of ASD, (b) having treatment manuals, (c) providing treatment with a high degree of intensity, and

2. measuring the overall effectiveness of the program. These treatment programs might also be referred to as ABA programs or behavioral inclusive programs and early intensive behavioral intervention.

Differential Reinforcement

The implementation of reinforcing only the appropriate response (or behavior to increase) and applying extinction to all other responses. Extinction is the discontinuing of a reinforcement of a previously reinforced behavior.

Discrete Trial Teaching (DTT)

A method of teaching in which the adult uses adult-directed, massed trial instruction, reinforcers chosen for their strength, and clear contingencies and repetition to teach new skills. DTT is a particularly strong method for developing a new response to a stimulus.

Exercise

Studies show that vigorous or strenuous exercise is associated with decreases in stereotypic (self-stimulatory) behaviors, hyperactivity, aggression, self-injury, and destructiveness. Vigorous exercise means a 20-minute or longer aerobic workout, three to four days a week; mild exercise has little effect on behavior. Many autistic children gain weight if they have an inactive lifestyle, and weight gain brings another set of problems.

Extinction

Extinction procedures apply the "principle of extinction," which proposes that because behaviors occur for a reason—we get things we want—if we stop getting what we want after we engage in a certain behavior, then that behavior will eventually stop occurring because it no longer serves any purpose.

Functional Behavior Assessment

These assessments are typically, but not exclusively, used to identify the causes of challenging behaviors, such as self-injury, aggression toward others, and destructive behaviors. Although there are different methods for carrying out functional assessments, they all have the same goal: to identify the function of a challenging behavior so that an intervention can be put in place to reduce this behavior and/or increase more adaptive behaviors.

Internally and Externally Motivated Behavior: Automatic Reinforcement versus External Reinforcement of Behavior

a. *To obtain the desired event:* internal stimulation or to obtain a social event; attention or activities/objects

b. *To escape or avoid in undesirable event:* to escape/avoid internal stimulation or to escape/avoid social events; attention or activities/objects

Functional Communication Training

Functional communication training (FCT) is most frequently used to replace interfering behaviors (for example, disruptive, repetitive/stereotypical) or subtle, less clear communicative forms (for example, reaching, leading) with more conventional communicative forms (for example, pointing, picture exchange, signing, verbalizations).

Joint Attention Intervention

These interventions involve building foundational skills involved in regulating the behaviors of others. Joint attention often involves teaching a child to respond to the nonverbal social bids of others or to initiate joint attention interactions.

Examples include pointing: to objects, showing items/activities to another person, and following eye gaze.

Modeling

These interventions rely on an adult or peer providing a demonstration of the target behavior that should result in an imitation of the target behavior by the individual with ASD. Modeling can include simple and complex behaviors. This intervention is often combined with other strategies, such as prompting and reinforcement. Examples include live modeling and video modeling.

Naturalistic Teaching Strategies

These interventions involve using primarily child-directed interactions to teach functional skills in the natural environment. These interventions often involve providing a stimulating environment, modeling how to play, encouraging conversation, providing choices and direct/natural reinforcers, as well as rewarding reasonable attempts.

Examples of this type of approach include, but are not limited to: focused stimulation, incidental teaching, milieu teaching, embedded teaching, as well as responsive education and pre-linguistic milieu teaching.

Parent-Implemented Intervention

Parent-implemented intervention includes programs in which parents are responsible for carrying out some or all the intervention(s) with their own child. Professionals train parents one-on-one, in group formats, or in home or community settings. Methods for training parents vary, but might include didactic instruction, discussions, modeling, coaching, or performance feedback. Parents might be trained to teach their child new skills, such as communication, play or self-help, and/or to decrease challenging behavior. Once parents are trained, they proceed to implement all or part of the intervention(s) with their child.

Peer Training Package

These interventions involve teaching children without disabilities strategies for facilitating play and social interactions with children on the autism spectrum. Peers often include classmates or siblings. When both initiation training and peer training were components of treatment in a study, the study was coded as "peer training package." These interventions might include components of other treatment packages (for example, self-management for peers, prompting, reinforcement). Common names for intervention strategies include peer networks, circle of friends, buddy skills package, Integrated Play Groups™, peer initiation training, and peer-mediated social interactions.

Picture Exchange Communication System

A form of augmentative and alternative communication.

Pivotal Response Treatment

This treatment is also referred to as PRT, Pivotal Response Teaching, and Pivotal Response Training. PRT focuses on targeting "pivotal" behavioral areas, such as motivation to engage in social communication, self-initiation, self-management, and responsiveness to multiple cues. The development of these areas is pursued while having the goal of widespread and fluently integrated collateral improvements. Key aspects of PRT intervention delivery also focus on parent involvement in the intervention delivery, and on intervention in the natural environment, such as homes and schools, with the goal of producing naturalized behavioral improvements. This method is considered by the American Academy of Pediatrics as favorable for its generalization over DTT. This treatment is an expansion of the natural language paradigm, which is also included in this category.

Prompting

A prompt can be defined as a cue or hint meant to induce a person to perform a desired behavior.

Reinforcement

The process of encouraging or establishing a belief or pattern of behavior, especially by encouragement or reward.

Response Interruption/Redirection (RIR)

This is an evidence-based practice used to decrease interfering behaviors, predominantly those that are repetitive, stereotypical, and self-injurious in nature. RIR is particularly useful with persistent, interfering behaviors that occur in the absence of other people, in a number of different settings, and during a variety of tasks. These behaviors often are not maintained by attention or escape.

Schedules

These interventions involve the presentation of a task list that communicates a series of activities or steps required to complete a specific activity. Schedules are often supplemented by other interventions, such as reinforcement. Schedules can take several forms, including written words, pictures or photographs, or workstations. For example, PECS.

Scripting

Script language is a programming language that supports scripts, programs written for a special run-time environment that automate the execution of tasks that could alternatively be executed one-by-one by a human operator.

Self-Management

These interventions involve promoting independence by teaching individuals with ASD to regulate their behavior by recording the occurrence/nonoccurrence of the target behavior, and securing reinforcement for doing so. Initial skills development might involve other strategies and include the task of setting one's own goals. In addition, reinforcement is a component of this intervention with the individual with ASD independently seeking and/or delivering reinforcers.

Examples include: the use of checklists (using checks, smiley/frowning faces), wrist counters, visual prompts, and tokens.

Social Narratives

Devised as a tool to help individuals on the autism spectrum better understand the nuances of interpersonal communication, so that they can interact in an effective and appropriate manner.

Social Skills Training

A behavioral approach for teaching preschool children age-appropriate social skills and competencies, including communication, problem solving, decision making, self-management, and peer relations.

Story-Based Intervention Package

These treatments involve a written description of the situations under which specific behaviors are expected to occur. Stories might be supplemented with additional components (for example, prompting, reinforcement, discussion). Social Stories™ are the most well-known, story-based interventions and they seek to answer the "who," "what," "when," "where," and "why" in order to improve perspective taking.

Structured Play Groups (SPG)

An intervention that uses small group activity to teach a broad range of outcomes. SPG activities are usually done for a defined area and activity. The goal is to move children with autism from a repetitive, solitary pattern of play to one that involves interaction and imagination.

Task Analysis

The process of learning about ordinary users by observing them in action to understand in detail how they perform their tasks and achieve their intended goals.

Technology-Aided Instruction and Intervention

These include technology as the central feature of an intervention that supports the goal or outcome for the student.

Time Delay

This is a procedure to increase spontaneous speech.

Video Modeling

This intervention technique is often used for social skills training, which involves participants watching a video of someone modeling a desired behavior and then imitating the behavior of the person in the video.

Visual Supports

Refers to using a picture or other visual item to communicate with a child who has difficulty understanding or using language.

CHAPTER 6

What Is Applied Behavioral Analysis in Autism?

"If today were the last day of your life, would you want to do what you are about to do today?"

— STEVE JOBS

Applied behavior analysis (ABA) is the use of techniques and principles to bring about meaningful and positive change in behavior for those diagnosed with autism, albeit accurate or flawed. It is currently the most commonly prescribed intervention for autism, along with minimal speech therapy, occupational therapy, and physical therapy.

Behavior analysis focuses on the principles that explain how learning takes place. Positive reinforcement is one such principle. When some sort of reward follows a behavior, the behavior is more likely to be repeated. Through decades of research, the field of behavior analysis has developed many techniques for increasing useful behaviors and reducing those that might cause harm or interfere with learning. It is not only beneficial, but also is extremely powerful when incorporated with RPM and AAC, just as PRT currently does.

Main Types of ABA

Discrete Trial Training (DTT)

Discrete trial training (DTT) is a component of most ABA programs for children with developmental delays. There is strong evidence that these techniques can produce rapid gains. DTT consists of a series of repeated lessons or broken-down trials taught 1:1. For younger children, we often begin with a series of brief, simple trials that build on skills and help to increase attention span, focus, and compliance. DTT encourages motivation by rewarding certain behaviors with external reinforcements, such as praise, edibles, toys, extra time to play, and so forth. Random rotating with error stimulates brain functioning and memory. Tell-ask procedures are important for all learning because it addresses working memory.

Pivotal Response Training (PRT)

Pivotal response training (PRT) is used to teach behaviors that are central to broad areas of functioning. Rather than target specific behaviors one at a time, PRT focuses on pivotal behaviors that can lead to improvements in other areas of behavior. Strengths of pivotal response training are enhanced internal motivation. Children with developmental delays typically lack the motivation to learn new tasks and participate in their social environment, which might be observed as temper tantrums, crying, fidgeting, staring, noncompliance, inattention, or lethargy.

PRT targets motivation through internal reinforcements by encouraging the child to respond to increasing expectations related to communication and socialization. Methods such as turn-taking, child choice, modeling, shaping, and direct reinforcement are emphasized. This method is more child-led, in that the child plays a central role in determining what activities and objects will be used for reinforcement during a PRT session.

Pivotal behaviors should be assessed. Behaviors that are considered pivotal and highly influential should be addressed first. Pivotal behaviors targeted must include motivation and attention. The Koegel Autism Center located at the University of California, Santa Barbara, offers certification in PRT. Pivotal behaviors should also include teaching a child how to acquire mand, tact, echoic, and intraverbal communication.

To teach fluency-based instruction, we must also assess the child's strengths based on standard knowledge of learning modalities: visual, auditory, tactile, kinesthetic, and olfactory. When teaching fluency-based instruction, it is imperative the child must be attending through their dominant learning modalities. Make sure the child has scanned the answer choices before choosing. They must know what they are choosing or the response is void. To ensure they scan the choices, prior to allowing them to choose the answer, gently restrain their hands before giving them the opportunity to choose.

The Difference between DTT and PRT

Both pivotal response training (PRT) and discrete trial training (DTT) incorporate the major principles of ABA to teach specified behaviors to individuals with developmental delays. DTT is more highly structured and is useful for teaching specific behavioral skills. PRT uses a less structured, more play-based format to develop skills and utilizes discrete trials as needed. Employing a blended model of the therapies to meet individualized needs is crucial.

Introducing Rapid Prompting Training (RPT) to Educational Curriculum

Many children with autism and intellectual disabilities need assistance developing independent typing skills to communicate measuring progress with evidence-based, assessment tools analyzing verbal operant skills according to applied behavioral methodologies. The dilemma is prompt dependency results. The goal of RPT is to reduce prompt dependency and foster independent learning, verbal expression, and social exchanges in the areas of verbal behaviors: mand, tact, intraverbal, and echoic. This methodological comprehensive training guide teaches learning, language, attention, motor skills, working memory skills, learning, visual perception, and cognitive processing skills to nonverbal, echoic, and minimally verbal students with autism spectrum disorders and intellectual disabilities.

General Management Guidelines of Applied Behavioral Analysis

Organizing the setting and carefully planning the approach can increase opportunities for successful learning and decrease the chances of a behavioral episode.

Set Goals: Setting goals gives a guideline to follow. It also gives our children the knowledge to know what we expect of them. It also allows them to have a sense of inclusion and control in times they feel out of control.

Over-plan: Be prepared on how you will handle behavior problems, ranging from noncompliance, escape, or physical aggression.

Task analyze: Break tasks down into smaller, highly descriptive steps. For example, the simple act of greeting someone at the door can be broken down into several smaller and more manageable steps.

Determine Environment: People with disorders requiring ABA are easily over-stimulated by their surroundings and require their therapeutic environment to be simple and quiet.

Simple Instruction: Simple and concrete instructions, prompts, and cues are important.

Consistent Instruction: The instructions must be based on the child's established abilities to communicate. Keep instructions consistent with this. If a child can match words to pictures or can auditorily choose correct choices, stay consistent with that to build on.

Model Behavior: We must model calm, consistent non-threatening behavior to our children who might feel threatened or display behavioral problems.

Provide Positive Feedback: All our children rely on their therapists to provide encouraging feedback until the ability being taught is learned.

Natural Reinforcers: Reinforcement should be given immediately and consistently where the child chooses the reinforcer, whether it is a stimulatory behavior or not (that is, jumping, spinning, blowing bubbles, opening and closing a door). The reinforcer is occurring within a natural setting and not in a tabletop-like structured environment.

Provide Choices: A crucial component to reducing serious behavior problems is offering control by giving choices.

Reduce Opportunities to Fail: Do not work on tasks above the child's level of ability, especially when establishing rapport. This increases a sense of failure leading to frustration and behavioral episodes. A success rate above 80 percent is generally expected when using operant conditioning. A feeling of success during trials while teaching new concepts is important.

Keep It Eclectic: Vary the therapy approaches intermittently to maintain interest and increase success. Play therapy, emotionally focused therapy, and cognitive behavioral therapy are alternatives.

Basic Behavioral Principles

Operant Conditioning Techniques

Positive Reinforcement: the adding of an appetitive stimulus to increase a certain behavior or response. Example: Father gives candy to his daughter when she picks up her toys. If the frequency of picking up the toys increases or stays the same, the candy is a positive reinforcement.

Negative Reinforcement: the taking away of an aversive stimulus to increase certain behaviors or responses. Example: Turning off distracting music when trying to work. If the work increases when the music is turned off, turning off the music is a negative reinforcement.

Positive Punishment: the adding of an aversive stimulus to decrease a certain behavior or response. Example: Mother yells at a child when running into the street. If the child stops running into the street, the yelling is positive punishment.

Negative Punishment (Omission Training): the taking away of an appetitive stimulus to decrease a certain behavior. Example: A teenager comes home an hour after curfew and the parents take away the teen's cell phone for two days. If the frequency of coming home after curfew decreases, the removal of the phone is negative punishment.

	Decreases likelihood of behavior	Increases likelihood of behavior
Presented	Positive punishment	Positive reinforcement
Taken away	Negative punishment	Negative reinforcement

Classical Conditioning: the conditioned stimulus (the sound of a bell) is paired with and precedes the unconditioned stimulus (the sight of food) until the conditioned stimulus alone is sufficient to elicit the response (salivation in a dog). The components of a person's "behavioral condition" are the antecedent, behavior, and consequence. These are known as the A-B-Cs of behavior analysis. Behavior analysis attempts to explain the relationship between these components.

Antecedent: The components of a person's behavioral condition are the antecedent, the behavior itself, and the consequence. Behavior analysis attempts to explain the relationship among these components. All behaviors to be modified are proceeded by some event in the person's environment. The preceding event is called the antecedent. The antecedent might be external, such as lighting, noise or verbal instructions or internal, such as headache, flu, seizure, or medication. Certain antecedents, such as during therapy, are part of the rehabilitative process and should not be avoided.

Behavior: An antecedent event is followed by the occurrence of a behavior. Individuals with traumatic brain injury can exhibit a number of maladaptive behaviors. Behavior disorders can be categorized as those occurring too often (in excess), those not occurring often enough (in deficit), and those not occurring in the correct context.

Consequence: Behaviors are followed by a consequence that will affect the future rate, duration, and intensity of the behavior. Consequences are either reinforcing or punishing. Reinforcers will increase and punishers will decrease the future occurrence of the behavior. Reinforcement programs should be tried before implementing a punishment program. Reinforcement programs teach people what to do and are generally more effective for long-term maintenance of the desired behavior.

Functions of Behaviors: Functions of behavior have been broken down into four categories. It is helpful to examine a child's function of behavior so goals will properly be developed. The four classified functions of behaviors are attention-seeking, escape, to gain access to something, and stimuli.

Reinforcement Program

Reinforcement: any stimulus that maintains or increases behavior exhibited immediately prior to the presentation of the stimulus. Reinforcement increases target behavior.

1. Positive Reinforcement—presentation of a stimulus.
2. Negative Reinforcement—removal of a stimulus (not the quality of the stimulus).

Effective use of reinforcements includes the following.

1. Immediacy of reinforcement
2. Combining verbal praise
3. Schedule of reinforcement
4. Type of reinforcement
5. Quality/quantity of reinforcement

Types of reinforcement include the following.

1. Primary Reinforcers—stimuli that are naturally reinforcing to individuals, such as food, warmth, etc.

2. Secondary Reinforcers—stimuli that are not naturally reinforcing—their value has been learned or conditioned, such as pairing verbal praise with a reward snack.

3. Socially Valid Reinforcers—in sync with the student's social setting (age, culture, relationship, etc.).

4. Identifying Reinforcers—high preference, most effective

5. Preference and Reinforce Assessment—assess what is most preferred and what is the influence on behavior.

6. Satiation—students become satiated when the same reinforcer is used too frequently.

Schedule of Reinforcement

1. Refers to the frequency or timing of the delivery of reinforcement following behavior.

   a. Ratio reinforcement schedules—based on established number of occurrences of the target behavior.

      i. Fixed ratio—every time the target behavior occurs.

      ii. Variable ratio—average number of occurrences.

   b. Interval reinforcement schedules—based on established interval of time, contingent on target behavior.

      i. Fixed interval schedule—reinforced after a specific interval of time.

      ii. Variable interval schedule—average interval of time.

Importance of Parental Involvement

Working together as a team is important for children's progress. Making sure that we all understand and consistently implement accurate behavioral procedures is in the team member and child's best interests.

ABA generally takes place in a restricted environment. The goal of behavior programs is for the client to be able to generalize behaviors learned in the clinic to other settings. For example, learning to control physical aggression in the clinic should be reflected in the ability to control aggression in the community.

2. Refers to the degree to which a behavior change transfers to other settings, situations, or behaviors.

   a. Stimulus generalization—describes the degree of behavior change in settings or situations other than training setting.

   b. Response generalization—refers to the degree to which a behavior change program influences other behaviors in addition to the target behavior.

3. Promoting Generalization

   a. Teach in natural setting—one in which behavior is most likely to occur.

   b. Natural antecedents—events or situations that should act as natural prompts or cues for specific behavior (teacher reads—students stop talking).

   c. Can pair artificial prompts with natural stimuli and fade them as soon as possible (ring bell before reading).

   d. Natural consequences—fade artificial consequences (from tokens to praise).

4. Promoting Maintenance of Behavior Change
   a. Teach where behavior is likely to occur (not pull-outs). Use a variety of teachers across multiple settings.
   b. Gradually shift from artificial stimulus controls to natural ones.
   c. Shift from continuous to intermittent schedules of reinforcement.
   d. Phase out artificial reinforcers.
   e. Introduce delays in the provision of reinforcers.
   f. Keep reinforcing generalization and maintenance.

Behavior Plan Format

A behavior treatment program includes four major components. These include short-term and long-term goals, definitions of target behaviors, data collection, and staff procedures.

Behavior treatment goals are separated into short-term and long-term goals. Short-term goals help the client and staff focus on tangible achievements. Long-term goals are the projected functional outcomes of the treatment, such as independent living skills or vocational placement.

Target behaviors are the focus of the treatment plan. These are the behaviors that interrupt therapy, impede progress, endanger others, disrupt activities, or otherwise interfere with a person's ability to live independently.

Each target behavior must be operationally defined. The operational definition describes what the behavior looks like in objective, observable terms.

The data collection system tracks the rate and duration of the target behavior. Without consistent data collection, it is difficult to ascertain whether the program is working.

The fourth, main section of the treatment plan describes the procedures of the program. It outlines how to arrange environmental conditions to reduce chances of behavioral episodes. The treatment plan also outlines response options to target behaviors.

Behavior Plan Procedures

There are many designs for behavior programs. Treatment procedures can be accelerative (those designed to increase the frequency or duration of a target behavior), decelerative (those designed to decrease the frequency or duration of a target behavior), or complex (those having characteristics of both accelerative and decelerative programs).

Accelerative programs involve positive programming, shaping, and chaining.

1. Positive programming is nothing more than teaching individuals new skills through the use of reinforcing consequences. Activities of daily living, functional communication, and social skills training are all examples of positive programming.

2. Shaping teaches gradual approximations of a target behavior. For example, teaching someone to be able to get his arm into the sleeve when learning to put on a shirt.

3. Chaining involves teaching the whole sequence of steps to a task. For example, teaching each step of the sequence required to put on a shirt.

Decelerative programs involve several different reinforcement procedures.

1. Differential reinforcement of incompatible behaviors (DRI) involves reinforcing behaviors that are different from, or incompatible with, the target behavior. For example, keeping one's hands in one's lap is incompatible with hitting oneself.

2. Differential reinforcement of other behaviors (DRO) reinforces any behavior other than the target behavior for a specific interval of time. For example, reinforcers are given for a specific time interval during which physical aggression is not exhibited.

3. Differential reinforcement of low rates of behavior (DRL) reinforces behaviors if a specified period of time has elapsed since the behavior last occurred, or if there have been only a specified number of episodes during a particular interval. For example, if the behavior is yelling, the client is rewarded for each 15-minute interval that passes since the yelling occurred, or for each interval in which yelling occurs below a certain rate.

4. Differential reinforcement of alternative behaviors (DRA) is reinforcement of a more appropriate form of a targeted behavior (ask, instead of demand something).

5. Differential reinforcement of higher rates of behaviors (DRH) reinforces the small increases in the rate of target behavior.

There are two types of over-correction procedures: restitutional and positive practice.

1. Restitutional over-correction requires that a person return the environment to a state better than before his or her behavioral episode.

2. Positive practice over-correction requires repeated practice of an appropriate behavior.

Stimulus change is a sudden introduction of an unrelated stimulus that results in a temporary reduction of the behavior. For example, clapping once, loudly, while a client is yelling will redirect his attention and temporarily stop the yelling.

Stimulus satiation allows the person unrestricted access to the reinforcer of the behavior.

Time-out procedures are either non-seclusionary or exclusionary. Non-seclusionary time-out involves withdrawing attention from a person while remaining in his or her presence. Exclusionary time-out involves removing the person from the environment following a behavior episode.

Complex behavior programs involve contracting, stimulus control, and token economies.

1. Contracting is a written agreement between the client and another person.

   Stimulus control brings the target behavior under the control of a specific stimulus or set of conditions. Behaviors are brought under control by reinforcing the target behavior at the time and location where the behavior should naturally or acceptably occur. For example, raising your hand instead of blurting out answers or step-by-step ways to problem solve individually.

2. Token economies use reinforcers that the client earns and which can be traded later for something of value to the client.

   For example, poker chips awarded for positive behaviors can be traded for a trip to the movies.

   a. Token economy = symbolic reinforcement system

    i.   Identify the target behavior to be increased.

    ii. Identify the medium of exchange.

    iii. Identify the reinforcers the students will be able to buy with tokens earned.

    iv. Identify the price of each reinforcement.

    v. Pick time for exchange of tokens for reinforcement.

Specific Behavioral Reduction Strategies

1. Extinction—gradually reduces the frequency or intensity of a target behavior by withholding reinforcement from behavior that was previously reinforced.

2. Time-Out from Positive Reinforcement—contingent on inappropriate behavior. Can remove the student from the reinforcement or remove the reinforcement from the student.

    a. Non-exclusion time-out—student not removed from the reinforcing environment, but attention and other forms of reinforcement are taken from the student for a limited period of time.

       i.   Planned ignoring—removal of social attention.

       ii. Removal of specific reinforcers—taking away things such as food, toys, etc., for a limited time.

       iii. Time-out ribbons—good with young children—take ribbon, bracelet, etc., until behavior terminated.

    b. Exclusion time-out—physical removal of student from a reinforcing environment or activity for period of time.

       i.   Contingent observation time-out—remove to sideline (for example, penalty box).

       ii. Isolation time-out—remove student totally (for example, designated corner).

iii. Seclusion time-out—complete removal of student to separate room or cubicle.

3. Response cost—systematic removal (tokens, points, etc.) contingent on behavior—used with token economy, often with inappropriate reinforcers.

4. Restitution—return environment to state prior to behavior that changed it (for example, clean up your mess).

   a. Overcorrecting—vastly improved environment (clean whole room).

5. Positive practice—practice an appropriate behavior as a consequence for inappropriate.

6. Medications

7. Physical restraint contact—manual restraint, person-to-person mechanical restraint, use of some apparatus.

8. Corporal punishment—hitting with hand or object with intent to cause pain or injury.

Data Collection

Behavior programming requires a procedure for systematically recording and analyzing behavior data. Before beginning any behavior program, data should be collected on the person's target behaviors. Baseline data provides the behavior programmer and staff with a clear picture of the frequency of maladaptive behaviors. When possible, data should be collected throughout the entire day and evening—not just in structured settings.

Systematic collection and analysis of data is important in tracking the progress of a treatment plan. Collecting data on a consistent basis will provide the following.

1. Baseline information—provides staff with a clear picture of the frequency of behaviors prior to starting the program. This information will help dictate the design of the treatment plan.

2. Judging ongoing effectiveness—collecting and graphing behavior data is important in tracking the progress of the treatment plan. Modifications to the plan should be "data driven" and not based on anecdotal staff reports alone.

3. Feedback—data collection provides important information to family, staff, and the client, as well as those responsible for the child's well-being and/or funding.

There are many methods for collecting data. The three most common and practical methods are event recording, interval recording, and time-sample recording.

1. Event recording—the easiest recording system. The only requirement is to mark on a piece of paper each time a specific target behavior occurs. The drawback to event recording is that it can be difficult to judge when one occurrence of a behavior ends and another occurrence begins.

2. Interval recording—divides the observation period into equal time periods (for example, 15-minute intervals) and requires the person recording to mark whether or not the behavior occurred during each interval. It does not matter how many times the behavior occurred, only that it occurred at least once. This eliminates the task of judging the beginning and ending of a behavioral episode and/or tallying high-frequency behaviors.

3. Time-sample recording—similar to interval recording, except that it does not require constant attention by the person recording. Behavior is only periodically sampled. Observation periods are divided into specific times, at

which time the person recording marks the occurrence or nonoccurrence of the behavior.

Crisis Prevention and Intervention

Most disorders requiring intensive ABA are oftentimes combative and resistant to change. If a behavioral crisis situation does occur, clinicians should be equipped with techniques to calm the child. Decreasing the likelihood of injury to himself/herself or others is crucial. It is wise to include in the informed consent form signed by parents or guardians that some restraint techniques might be necessary.

To prevent a crisis situation, foremost, conduct a functional behavioral analysis. Make sure children have had enough rest time, reduce chaos, keep instructions simple, give feedback and set goals. Stay calm and redirect, provide choices, decrease the person's chance of failure, vary type of activities, over-plan, and use task analysis. Monitor body posture, tone of voice, content of speech, and use of gestures. There are many techniques for preventing a crisis situation or intervening once it has started.

If conflicts do escalate, a teacher/therapist must immediately intervene. Some of the most effective de-escalation techniques include active listening, orientation to time and place, setting limits, redirection, and extinction—withdrawal of attention. Calmly paraphrase and validate the child's feelings with direct directions of desired behavior. Staying calm and redirecting a child to another task or activity can also interrupt the escalation phase. Reminding the child of the time and place of the location might help. Sometimes a teacher/therapist must exit the room and seek assistance.

CHAPTER 7

What Is Cognitive Behavioral Therapy?

"The final forming of a person's character lies in their own hands."

— ANNE FRANK

Cognitive behavioral therapy is concerned with understanding how events and experiences are interpreted. Also of importance is identifying and changing the distortions or deficits that occur in cognitive processing. Cognitive behavioral therapy (CBT) is used primarily to help individuals with ASD regulate their emotions and develop impulse control, and improve their behavior as a result. In addition, some individuals with ASD struggle with fears and anxiety or might become depressed. Cognitive behavior therapy has been shown to be helpful for reducing anxious and depressed feelings and behavior by making changes in thoughts and perceptions of situations through a change in cognition. The key ingredient of CBT, which distinguishes it from regular behavior therapy, is working on this change in cognition or how thinking is processed.

CBT can be individualized for each patient, and as a result, is effective at improving specific behaviors and challenges in each child or young adult. Stabilizing emotions and improving behavior allows those with ASD to prepare for, and respond more appropriately to, specific situations. The CBT triangle (see example) is the symbol for how human behavior is understood through the lens of CBT. Each point in the triangle is connected to the others, the assumption being that any change on one point will cause change in the other two points.

The CBT Triangle

Examples of Cognitive Distortions

1. **All-or-Nothing Thinking:** viewing situations on one extreme or another instead of on a continuum. For example, "If my child does bad things, it is because I am a bad parent."

2. **Catastrophizing:** Predicting only negative outcomes for the future. For example, "If I fail my final, my life will be over"

3. **Disqualifying or Discounting the Positive:** Telling yourself that the good things that happen to you don't count. For example, "My daughter told her friend that I was the best dad in the world, but I am sure she was just being nice."

4. **Emotional Reasoning:** Feeling about something that overrules facts to the contrary. For example, "Even though Steve is here at work late every day, I know I work harder than anyone else at my job."

5. **Labeling:** Giving someone or something a label without finding out more about it/them. For example, "My daughter would never do anything I disapproved of."

6. **Magnification/Minimization:** Emphasizing the negative or downplaying the positive of a situation. For example, "My

professor said he made some corrections on my paper, so I know I'll probably fail the class."

7. **Mental Filter/Tunnel Vision:** Placing all your attention on the negatives of a situation or seeing only the negatives of a situation. For example, "My husband says he wished I was better at housekeeping, so I must be a lousy wife." "My daughter's boyfriend got suspended from school. He's a loser and won't ever amount to anything."

8. **Mind Reading:** Believing you know what others are thinking. For example, "My house was dirty when my friends came over, so I know they think I'm a slob."

9. **Overgeneralization:** Making an overall negative conclusion beyond the current situation. For example, "My husband didn't kiss me when he came home this evening. Maybe he doesn't love me anymore."

10. **Personalization:** Thinking the negative behavior of others has something to do with you. For example, "My daughter has been fairly quiet today. I wonder what I did to upset her."

11. **"Should" and "Must" Statements:** Having a concrete idea of how people should behave. For example, "I should get all A's to be a good student."

CHAPTER 8

Assistive Augmentative Technology's Role in Autism

"The problem is not the problem; the problem is your attitude about the problem."

— CAPTAIN JACK SPARROW

ASD can expand and improve social skills through training and special therapy with Assistive Augmentative Technology (AAT). Though children with ASD might have strong language skills, it is important that they learn how to express their thoughts and feelings appropriately. Their ability to interact with others can improve with lots of practice and explicit teaching. Therapists often teach social skills and speech to children using visual techniques such as social stories or using exercises that involve the children in various social situations. Speech and language therapy might also help these children to communicate better. This therapy could correct awkward methods of speaking, such as monotone, and help children to better understand and interpret the speech and communication signals of others, such as humor, eye contact, and hand gestures.

A typically developing child uses many single words before putting words together. Brown's Stages of Syntactic and Morphological Development for Language can be used as a guide.

Individuals diagnosed with autism are unable to verbally express feelings, thoughts, and needs. Their struggle to communicate even the most basic needs through gestures, facial expressions, and body language can be frustrating and frightening to these individuals and their families. The inability to communicate effectively often presents a barrier to learning and literacy and creates significant obstacles to social and emotional development and independence. Augmentative and Alternative Communication (AAC), also frequently called Speech Generating Devices (SGDs) or Voice Output Communication Aids (VOCAs), are devices that can provide a bridge from a life where thoughts, feelings, and needs are held in silence, to a life where interaction, expression and learning are possible.

"Augmentative communication devices and strategies help us understand that many people with autism have a broad range of feelings, interests, opinions and keen intellectual capacities," says Karen Kaye-Beall, director of the Augmentative Communication Showroom and Demonstration Center in Silver Spring, Maryland, where people with autism and their families can try out a wide variety of speech generating devices. "At their deepest core, people with autism are loving people who want to have close relationships with others. They just find it extremely difficult and confusing to express the thoughts and feelings that are locked up inside. Thus, developing and maintaining friendships is challenging and people with autism can often feel lonely and isolated as a result of their disabilities. People often misunderstand this and believe that individuals with autism want to be alone. In many instances, that is simply not true."

Why does ACC work so well for people with autism?

In a leading book on AAC by autism specialist Joanne Cafiero, *Meaningful Exchanges for People with Autism: An Introduction to Augmentative and Alternative Communication,* Dr. Cafiero talks about all the ways AAC fits people with autism well.

- Most people with autism are visual learners—AAC uses visual cues.

- Many people with autism are interested in inanimate objects—AAC tools and devices are inanimate.

- Many people with autism have difficulty with complex cues—level of complexity can be controlled so AAC grows with the child.

- Many people with autism have difficulty with change—AAC is static and predictable.

- Most people with autism have difficulty with the complexities of social interaction—AAC provides a buffer and bridge between communication partners.

- Some people with autism have difficulty with motor planning—AAC is motorically easier than speech.

- Many people with autism experience anxiety—AAC interventions don't apply pressure or stress (when introduced properly).

- Many people with autism present behavioral challenges—AAC provides an instant means to communicate, preempting difficult behaviors.

- Many people with autism have difficulty with memory—AAC provides a means for language comprehension that relies on recognition rather than memory.

- May stimulate brain development.
- Supports functional spontaneous communication.
- Facilitates access to social exchanges.
- Facilitates inclusion at home, school, and community.
- Facilitates greater independence in the home, school, and community.
- Facilitates access to literacy experiences.
- Preempts the need to develop dysfunction communicative behaviors (reduces meltdowns).
- Provides voice and ears to people with autism, including psychological benefits of better understanding others and being understood.
- Facilitates an improved sense of self-concept due to greater independence and fewer outbursts.

Is an augmentative communication device only appropriate for people who are nonverbal, or does it help with those who are verbal?

Speech-generating devices (SGDs) are programmed to provide a functional and effective vocabulary for any individual with communication problems, regardless of age or diagnosis. There are no cognitive, behavioral, or language prerequisites required for most augmentative communication interventions. Nearly anyone can benefit from augmentative communication tools and strategies when utilized properly.

SGDs are intended to enhance existing functional communication by:

1. Clarifying vocalizations, gestures, body language, etc.
2. Expanding the language of limited speakers by increasing their vocabulary to include verbs, descriptors, exclamatory comments, etc.

3. Replacing speech for people who are nonverbal.

4. Providing the structures and tools to develop language.

How do augmentative communication devices work?

With SGDs, a communicator just touches a labeled icon (which might be a picture communication symbol or some similar graphics) on the display screen of the device, and the device will say, out loud, the word, phrase, or sentence that the individual intends to express. You can set the "synthesized" (computer-generated) voice to sound like a boy or girl, or a man or woman's voice. You can also record your own voice or someone else's voice and this is referred to as a "digitized" voice recording.

Communicators need to communicate words and phrases that are most motivating and reinforcing to begin with and gradually add more and more vocabulary. Labeled icons (or buttons or cells) can be customized to each individual's unique choices so that an SGD can be personalized and more closely express each individual's wants and needs. For example, if a person touches the buttons for "I am hungry," the page might automatically change to display a full array of food and drink choices and condiments, as well as a wide variety of restaurant choices in the community. By offering an array of choices, the communicator is not taken to Taco Bell, when he or she really wanted to eat at McDonald's. The communicator can choose mustard, rather than ketchup, on his or her burger. Little choices like these matter.

What are the ranges of topics an AAC user can communicate about using an augmentative communication device?

With consistent practice and depending on the capability and sophistication of the SGD, a communicator can potentially express nearly anything he or she will need or want to express.

The basis of all communication is some type of language framework that must provide a vocabulary that is appropriate for the communicator's age and the multiple settings in which the person needs to communicate, such as at home, school, job sites, visits with friends and relatives, and more.

As adults, we normally have a speaking vocabulary of between 10,000 and 30,000 words, but a "core" of just 100 words accounts for approximately 50 percent of words spoken. Examples of such words include I, to, you, the, that, have, a, it, my, and, of, will, in, is, me, on, do, was, etc.

Most of the more sophisticated, or high-tech SGDs come already preprogrammed with 4,000+ words and/or icons. While there are variations between SGD vendors and devices, to be sure, most provide preset vocabulary choices or pages to expand vocabulary that express feelings/emotions; personal identifying information such as name, address, and phone; names of family members, friends, and other important people; actions of all sorts; possessions and toys for play; leisure activity choices, including sports, music, and more; places we visit in the community and geography; clothing choices; body parts and medical pages; calendars, clocks, holidays, and special occasions; daytime, evening, and weekend routines; arts and craft supplies, colors and shapes; commonly used social phrases, such as hello, goodbye, my name is, how much does this cost, etc. There are also many "word group" pages that provide extensive vocabulary for specific classes, such as animals, dinosaurs, vehicles, furniture, appliances, utensils, hygiene, jobs and occupations, tools, money, and more. You can even tell jokes and riddles using an AAC device.

The ultimate goal of AAC is spontaneous, novel communication; the ability to access individual words, expressions, and commonly used phrases; and to allow any individual at nearly any age, with any disability to say anything, talk about any subject, at any time.

AAC is never used to replace existing functional language, but rather to enhance it. The SGDs and their programs are intended to increase, maintain, or improve a person's ability to communicate by augmenting the skills he or she already possesses and providing alternative means when that degree of support is needed. Dr. Cafiero, in *Meaningful Exchanges for People with Autism,* reviews various studies and concludes the following: "There is no research-based evidence demonstrating that AAC interferes with the development of speech ... Research indicates that AAC actually facilitates speech by increasing communicative skills and interactions ... and provides models for speech prompts."

Since SGDs usually have visual symbols and/or icons paired with voice output, this combination has been proved successful with people with autism to increase communication. Case study research, although limited, shows that the more visual and verbal input received by a person with ASD, the more expressive language he or she will generate.

Research and clinical practice have shown that AAC systems do not interfere with speech development. In fact, many children demonstrate an increase in language, speech, and communication skills once an AAC system is introduced. In *Total Augmentative Communication in the Early Childhood Classroom,* Linda J. Burkhart proposed several reasons for this.

- Reduced pressure on speech production as the sole means of communication.
- Continued development of language skills.
- Continued development of conversational skills.
- Children will use the easiest method possible as their preferred means of communication. It is much easier for a child to use speech and/or vocalizations if possible to communicate than to formulate a message using an augmentative communication system.

Barriers to some products and applications using AAT is the child's obsession to engage in self-stimulatory behaviors. Conflicts between pressing buttons over and over or escaping the program to rewind and fast forward should be avoided. The interconnectivity of the brain becomes strengthened the more we do something. Therefore, if we want our children to improve communication and social interactivity it is highly recommended to use a paper version if self-stimulatory behavior impedes progress or increases impeding behaviors.

CHAPTER 9

What Is ESP's Role?

Dominic and I have witnessed amazing miracles and dispelled many untruths over decades about autism's *cant's* versus *cans*. In addition to helping Dominic, my patients, and students communicate their brilliance and progress in their learning capabilities against all odds, I have discovered that ESP has also been factually documented among a few children. Many of us have read *The Indigo Children* by Lee Carroll and Jan Tober in hopes of better understanding the uniqueness and gifts of our children while our own sanity is questioned by mainstream science. The brain has survived and evolved in many different ways over thousands of years. It is quite explainable that humans may develop communication styles analogous to dolphins, horses, and dogs. The fact others have accused many of the professionals proving and studying the possibilities of ESP as "crazy" saddens us beyond description.

Dr. Diane Powell's book *ESP Enigma* is well respected by other well-educated doctors. Its testimonials state, "*The ESP Enigma* is a revolutionary explanation of the link between psychic phenomena and how human consciousness works. Dr. Diane Powell, a prominent Johns Hopkins–trained neuropsychiatrist, examines the evidence for many types of psychic phenomena, from telepathy and precognition to psychokinesis, and finds several well-designed and rigorously supervised studies that prove the existence of some psychic phenomena. The fact that psychic abilities are stronger among prodigies, autistic savants, and some people who are bipolar or have suffered certain brain injuries has led to brain-imaging and other research that can explain which parts of the brain are dominant in psychics and mystics. Dr. Powell proposes a new paradigm for consciousness that would explain psychic phenomena, such as how the mind of a mystic or psychic could have an organizational effect on the physical world. Grounded in decades of reliable scientific research, *The ESP Enigma* establishes a common ground among psychic phenomena believers and skeptics."

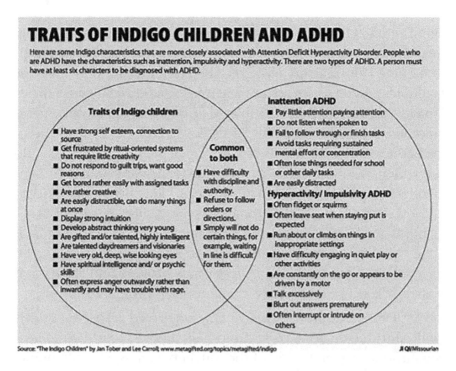

Source: "The Indigo Children" by Jan Tober and Lee Carroll, www.metagifted.org/topics/metagifted/indigo   JI QI/Missourian

Dominic and I decided to approach Dr. Diane Hennacy Powell, M.D. while doing our research at USC, working with Soma using the Rapid Prompting Method, the 2016 documentary film *Vaxxed*, an ABC news reporter, the Akhil Autism Foundation, Dr. Shazia Hyder, M.D., Dr. Gabriella Lesmo, and Hope, Inc.'s prior vice president, Dr. Taif Kaissi, M.D. Our family has studied the possibility of ESP and savants beginning in the '50s when my grandfather, mother, and Native American aunt exerted its validity. My grandmother, an editor for NASA, and my great uncle, an attorney writing for the New York Times, also studied its legitimacy. In the Bible, the many gifts God bestows us is vast and possible.

Due to all the corruption and false allegations, we needed independent validation from someone with similar research on ESP, savant abilities, and accurate learning potentials. The legal evidence, school records, medical charts, and bank accounts all indicated the truth about what children and their families are subjected to, but I never thought our own lives would become so unmanageable so quickly once enrolling at USC while engaged in hostile divorce. My children, patients, and students were all now victims of their own father from the LAPD, the Glendora Police Department, an unidentified criminal who stole our advocacy data, research, and experimental videos splicing them up mailing them to the State of California, a lieutenant from LAPD's company Global 360, who we hired to protect all of us, and dishonest social workers. My own mental stability and prescription use due to the years of torment began to unravel the fabric of our family.

Considering we were the first to prove ESP and the ability for children to independently type with coherent, brilliant thoughts on video with countless M.D.s, clinicians, educators, and therapists present to witness such abilities, we hired Dr. Powell to co-author this book, validate our research, evaluating and treating patients and students. There are endless pieces of trial paperwork, audio and video evidence, attesting to the last two decades of our assertive claims.

Nonetheless, Dominic has asked for his report to be shared for the world to see like many of his others. I have and will always respect my son's requests to utilize him as a witness to the possibility of hope against all odds. Dominic and I have no problem with transparency, accountability, and outcomes. Our intentions are for humanity, civil justice, and world peace above all costs.

DIANE HENNACY

Powell, M.D

245 Valley View Drive

Medford, OR 97504

541-770-3171

PSYCHIATRIC EVALUATION
(Confidential)

Name: Dominic S. Juarez

Date of Birth: October 5, 2000

Age: 15

Referred by: Taif Kassi, M.D.

Place of Examination: Glendora, CA

Dates of Examination: June 8, 2016, June 9, 2016, and June 10, 2016

Date of Report: August 17, 2017

Examiner: Diane Hennacy Powell, M.D.

Reason for Referral:

The reason for referral was clarification of diagnosis, to assist in treatment planning, and to determine whether Dominic is capable of independent typing skills, which would enable him to communicate and progress academically.

Background Information:

Complete medical records were not available, but the following sources were obtained and appear to be reliable. They include: medical records from Dr. Gabriella Lesmo, Michael Goldberg, MD, and Dana Wyss, M.S. LMFT, interviews with Dominic's family (mother Jamie Juarez and his sisters), and observation during six RPM sessions with Soma Mukhopadhyay.

Identifying information: Dominic is a 15-year-old Hispanic/Italian/Native American male student diagnosed with severe autism, chronic fatigue, fibromyalgia, epilepsy, sensory processing disorder, OCD, and viral encephalitis. His mother reports he was developing normally until immediately after receiving routine vaccinations at round age one. Since then he has had the following presenting complaints and symptoms: "anxiety, hyperactivity, impulsivity, social deficits, sensory deficits, developmental delays, intellectual delays, and expressive/receptive language delays." He cannot prepare his own meals, brush his teeth independently, tie his shoes, nor properly wipe himself when using the bathroom. His diet is gluten-free. His sleep cycles vary from insomnia to hypersomnia. He has had grand mal seizures daily, but now they occur monthly.

Family History: Psychiatric problems in the family history include a brother with oppositional/conduct disorder and a mother with an unclear diagnosis. She was involuntarily hospitalized because her beliefs were judged as psychotic delusions. She was diagnosed with bipolar I disorder and ADHD, but believes her diagnosis should be post-traumatic stress disorder.

Dominic's mother is an LMFT in a doctoral program in education at USC, and his father is a police officer. The parents are divorced. According to his mother, Dominic communicates regularly with his letter board while with her, but his father rarely uses it with him.

There is no history of substance abuse.

Medications tried include: Celexa, Prozac, Zoloft, Wellbutrin, Strattera, Adderall, Lamictal, Nizoral, Tenex, Valtrex, Acyclovir, and Diflucan.

Behavioral Observations:

Dominic is a large, well-developed boy who appeared alert, but tired. When not actively engaged, he lays on the floor with a blanket completely covering him, including his face. He was also in a wheelchair much of the time due to ankle pain. His speech is relatively nonexistent and poorly articulated. He occasionally grunts and says only a few words. No echolalia was observed. He was very cooperative when communicating with a letter board with his mother, sister Danielle, and Soma. Although some of his answers display a sense of humor, his facial expression does not vary, usually looking frown-like. When called, he responds to his name, gets off the floor, and brings his blanket with him. To answer questions, he rapidly points to letters on a letter board or types on a keyboard. His answers were coherent and relevant, suggesting his language comprehension vastly exceeds his capacity for expression.

Examples of Dominic's writings include:

"I want to take advanced classes and travel the world to write about different experiences."

"My favorite subject has now become history when it was rather science before. I feel like science is corrupted and the only way to make change is historical."

"I think I can grow a beard if I wanted to."

"My body feels like it is on fire. I can't control it even though my mind wants to. Living in my body and mind feels like hell on earth."

"Others think I am dumb, but I am not. I just process different and my mom and Soma helped figure it out first."

There was no evidence found in his behavior for suicidal or violent ideation. Nor was there any evidence of delusional thinking or hallucinations. Based upon his cooperative and attentive behavior, this is likely to be an accurate assessment of his current potential for communication. However, his full potential is probably much higher.

Summary:

Although Dominic was initially diagnosed as mentally retarded, he appears to have average to above average intellectual functioning. He suffers from a severe impairment of speech, but he successfully demonstrated his ability to express his thoughts on a letter board and/or keyboard. He did not display some of the characteristic signs of autism spectrum disorder, which is his current diagnosis.

For example, his emotional and social desires appear to be typical of other children his age. He was not observed to engage in any complex ritualistic behaviors. He also did not have the excessive need for sameness described by Dr. Leo Kanner in his description of autism.

His current symptoms can be explained by an encephalopathy, which has impaired his ability to express himself, which in turn impacts normal social development. He also has obsessive-compulsive disorder (OCD), and autoimmune conditions are known to be one of their causes. Based upon the information provided, Dominic's primary diagnoses would be encephalopathy, with the secondary diagnoses of sensory processing disorder and obsessive-compulsive disorder.

Autism spectrum disorder (ASD) is a syndrome that has many genes associated with it and is believed to have many medical causes. Based upon his history, Dominic's ASD would be secondary to the encephalopathy. His behavior has improved as a result of treatment with antivirals and learning a means to communicate. Some children can improve so that the diagnosis of ASD no longer is accurate. This might or might not be the case for Dominic.

Diagnosis:

Axis I: F84.0 autistic disorder, F42 obsessive-compulsive disorder

Axis II: None

Axis III: Seizure disorder, viral encephalitis versus autoimmune encephalopathy

Axis IV: Extreme: health issues, conflicts between parents, visits from Child Protective Services, brother who bullies him

Axis V: GAF Current: 15

GAF Highest in past year: 15

Recommendations:

Dominic requires regular access to his means of communication, which is via a letter board and/or keyboard. This is necessary not only for the purposes of his obtaining an education, but also for interacting successfully with others, including medical professionals and other students. Without more records, it is difficult to comment upon other aspects of his diagnosis and treatment.

Respectfully submitted,

_____

Diane Hennacy Powell, MD Psychiatrist

- Chen, G M, Yoder, KJ, et al, "Harnessing repetitive behaviors to engage attention and learning in a novel therapy for autism: an exploratory analysis," *Frontiers in Psychology*, February 2012, volume 3, Article 12, 1-16.
- Gutman, SA, Raphael-Greenfield, et al, "Using motor-based role-play to enhance social skills in a nonverbal adolescent with high functioning autism: a case report, *Occupational Therapy in Mental Health*, 30:1, 12-25.

- Kanner L. "Autistic disturbances of affective contact." *Nervous Child*, 1943, 2, 217-250.

- Rogers, SJ, Hayden, D., et al, "Teaching young nonverbal children with autism useful speech: a pilot study of the Denver model and PROMPT interventions" *J Autism Dev Disorders*, July 2006, 36: 1007-1024.

- Turner, MA, Hammond, N. "Cognitive behavioral therapy in the treatment of social skills deficits and social phobia in a man with autism spectrum disorder: a single case study." *The Cognitive Behaviour Therapist*, 2006, Volume 9, e3, 1-15.

CHAPTER 10

What Is the Rapid Prompting Training's "Your Child Can Type?"

"A treatment method or an educational method that will work for one child may not work for another child. The one common denominator for all of the young children is that early intervention does work, and it seems to improve the prognosis."

—TEMPLE GRANDIN, PROFESSOR AT COLORADO STATE UNIVERSITY

AND PERSON WITH AUTISM

"We found hope for our son with Hope for Autism! The founder and executive director of her son's nonprofit Jamie Juarez's Your Child Can Type program proved to us in less than two weeks that our son, diagnosed mentally retarded and nonverbal, severely autistic, self-injurious, and aggressive could independently type on a computer keyboard with no physical prompts. He miraculously demonstrated his learning capabilities, emotional connections, and savant skills to us, family, friends, and independent experts indicating this was not 'autism.' Our beautiful son went from extremely misunderstood to incredibly understood with quality and ethics based services provided by Jamie Melillo Juarez. None of this would have been possible without Your Child Can Type!"

—SHAZIA HYDER, MD

"Jamie Melillo Juarez's Your Child Can Type program has provided the most exceptional educational services to my autistic son that changed and forever improved his quality of life. Her program's services included so much, but the neuropsychological and psychosocial assessments, non-public school placement with highly effective autism protocols and various testing recommendations she made changed our lives. She brought to light an auditory processing disorder and ligament condition that prevented my 12-year-old from writing, but was finally treated. He has improved his working memory and grasp of academic grade levels indescribably. The opportunity for my son to work with Jamie is always a life-changing opportunity to never pass up. Your Child Can Type is simply one of Jamie's genius out-of-the-box approaches to education and therapy that always works for my son and all the countless families I know who have benefitted from her programs. I highly recommend giving your child a renewed confidence in themselves by taking the Your Child Can Type program."

—RAINA BEAVEN, SPECIAL EDUCATION ADVOCATE

My son was fortunate enough to begin interventions from Jamie at 8 years old in 2009. He was diagnosed as moderate to severe autism, non-verbal and we were told he would never speak. He slowly began to express himself with echoic, robotic speech, and had no ability to processing verbal information. Once he received Hope for Autism's services we quickly saw a child begin to express himself effectively, process information accurately, and complete academically challenging work. We were so blessed to have Jamie's interventions coach him into the verbal and high functioning teenager he is today.

-FLORA MARTINEZ, SPECIAL NEEDS ADVOCATE

Product Description

Rapid Prompting Training (RPT) "Your Child Can Type" is an innovative neuroscience-derived behavioral modification curriculum. It is psychophysiological, based on twenty years of evidence-based research with more than 700 subjects emphasizing verbal operant, psychotherapeutic perspectives designed specifically from meta-analyzed, evidence-based-and-emerging, evidence-based-and-promising practice methodologies. The application and physical products begin by teaching children visual motor pointing skills. This initial drag-and-drop approach establishes visual motor and phonetic integration necessary to type, equally paired with knowledge-based content and ease of skill. The child must drag and drop colors, numbers, activities, items, and emotions while receiving visual and auditory reinforcement for whole brain functioning. In proper sequential order of scientific, evidence-based learning processes, the child then engages in the more difficult tasks, calling on his or her prior visual, auditory, and sensory knowledge. The child must then recall the previously matched word by typing the correct corresponding letters from a simpler field choice of two letters. The visual and auditory field becomes larger and harder, stimulating informational processing, working memory, visual motor skills, and fluid attention.

Your Child Can Type: Keys to Unlocking Your Child's Voice is a neuroscience-based training program that teaches phonetic typing skills. Neuroscience and applied behavior analysis advancements show activating these areas of the brain are scientifically proven to increase attention, working memory, knowledge retrieval, information processing, and engagement that are crucial for advanced learning. This application software and physical product quickly teaches your child how to type, read, and spell.

Research indicates knowledge and motivation greatly improve by stimulating memory retrieval, sensory activation from both sides of the brain's hemispheres, and scaffolding visual motor skills with positive reinforcement. The interaction of these carefully designed phases in Your Child Can Type reinforces visual, auditory, and sensory-spatial dimensions improving informational processing, working memory, motor processing, and fluid intelligence, all crucial brain functioning processes scientifically proven to be correlated to high-performance learning.

During the past 20 years, Jamie has dedicated her professional and personal life to studying healthcare law, psychopharmacology, biomedicine, augmentative assistive technology, behavior modification, applied behavioral analysis, discrete trial training, verbal behavior, pivotal response training, video modeling, incidental teaching, Treatment and Education of Autistic and Related Communication Handicapped Children (TEACCH), cognitive behavior, existential humanism, neuroscience, neurofeedback, biofeedback, evolutionary psychology, relationship development intervention, Lindamood Phoneme Sequencing, Cogmed working memory, quantitative electroencephalographs, Fast ForWord, Brain Gym, and special education law. This methodological, comprehensive training guide teaches learning, language, attention, motor skills, working memory skills, learning, visual perception, and cognitive processing skills to nonverbal, echoic, and minimally verbal students with autism spectrum disorders and intellectual disabilities. The program can be utilized with all ages to improve working memory, typing, and new language acquisition.

Methodological Details of Rapid Prompting Training's (RPT) "Your Child Can Type"

Many children with autism and intellectual disabilities need assistance developing independent typing skills to communicate. This method measures progress with evidence-based assessment tools, analyzing verbal operant skills according to applied behavioral methodologies, visual and auditory-motor processing, and information processing for memory. The dilemma is prompt dependency results. The goal of RPT is to reduce prompt dependency and foster independent learning verbal expression, and social exchanges in the area of verbal behaviors: mand, tact, intraverbal, and echoic.

This training teaches generalized learning, communication, language, attention, motor skills, working memory, visual perception, and cognitive processing skills to nonverbal, echoic, and minimally verbal students with autism spectrum disorders and intellectual disabilities without long-term dependence on prompts and supports. For a professional working with autism, it is imperative to understand an array of evidence-based interventions, which is exactly why RPT methods are foundationally based on an eclectic perspective of meta-analyzed methods of success. The following research at Harvard is embedded in Rapid Prompting Training's *Your Child Can Type.*

We must redefine the accurate, reflective symptoms to achieve optimal, humanitarian functioning. The mindset that those with autism, ADHD, and other various intellectual disabilities learn more slowly or have ceilings of learning is simply erroneous. Individuals with autism and intellectual disabilities simply learn and express differently than the normative samples we have traditionally compared them to for decades. Neuroscience is proving this. They simply learn and express differently, and it is our job to innovate new ways of achieving success. We must have innovative methods for helping the epidemic proportions of autism, attention deficit hyperactivity, and intellectual disabilities occurring for the good of humanity, as well as for societal benefit. We want our future generations to prosper, be treated with integrity, and have equal opportunities, just like all neurotypical children. PRT rectifies this gap.

Behavioral analysis has been extremely beneficial for achieving learning, behavioral, and social-emotional successes. The use of applied behavioral analysis has its extreme benefits and is scientifically sound. However, we need new innovative, eclectic perspectives to increase the probabilities of optimal, rapid growth as the child's brain develops. Neuroscience-based methodologies based on brain plasticity integrated with applied behavioral analysis are the wave of the future. RPT does this for our children. Its foundation is grounded in brain science with decades of evidence-applied behavioral analysis to support it.

The ultimate goal of RPT, as a neuroscience derived applied behavior analysis model, is to foster independent learning, attention, and social skills with typing skills fostering optimal growth in the areas of verbal behaviors: mand, tact, intraverbal, and echoic, while reducing prompt dependency on teachers, therapists, and 1:1 aides. Psychologist B. F. Skinner defined verbal behavior as "behavior reinforced through the mediation of other persons." Verbal behavior is reinforced and develops within the environment of other verbal individuals. "Verbal" can include blowing a horn to get someone's attention, pulling a parent's hand to the refrigerator, speaking vocally, signing, using PECs, typing, or using gestures and facial expressions. There is an emphasis with RPT on producing generalized verbal behavior with typing so the child is motivated to learn independently, demonstrates intellectual readiness, participates in group instruction, develops working memory skills, and engages socially.

Individuals with ASD have unique spectrums of impairments in their language and motor development. Many children with autism and intellectual disabilities need assistance with developing communication, attending to curriculum, and developing typing skills to convey their thoughts. This ultimately leads to improved behavioral, learning, and social-emotional skills. Examination of a child's verbal operant abilities, as defined by Skinner, to accurately develop mand, tact, intraverbal, and echoic mastery is possible quickly with the use of a keyboard paired with 2D and 3D stimuli. Identifying a child's understanding of the alphabet's letters by use of pointing to a laminated keyboard is extremely powerful when identifying functional communication repertoires and teaching procedures to have the child produce verbal operants.

Impairments in their frontal and sensorimotor areas of the brain are one of the single most impacted development impeding learning, behavioral, and social-emotional growth. The delay in their lips and voice production is evident. The delay in their fine-motor and gross-motor skills is substantial. Visual motor attention and integration is equally an area of the brain heavily impacted. These particular developmental impedances can be rectified and their correction opens endless opportunities when beginning both a verbal, nonverbal, and emerging verbal individual with autism using a keyboard as a means of establishing successful mastery of all verbal operants during an ABA or academic program.

Conducting use of the keyboard with matching and fading strategies in multiple natural and contrived environments, while engaged in a variety of calming, unimposing, excitatory visual, auditory, and sensory-based activities facilitate motivation, creates independence, reduces prompt dependency, and improves generalization of mastery. Understanding what motivates a child to communicate with the keyboard increases the child's motivation to engage during behavior and communication acquisition.

The keyboard, when offered fields of two, initially motivates a child to integrate his or her brain functioning, thus keeping the default network system deactivated and the task-positive network activated by scanning for choices, focusing attentively, and employing impacted motor skills. Videotaping the child while using the keyboard, with fields of two initially, and then playing it back for him or her to see, equally stimulates the child's brain, interest, motivation, and attending skills.

There are two types of motivation: internal and external. Internal motivations are generally more powerful than external, evolving from naturally occurring primary reinforcements, such as food and water. External motivation is powerful as well. However, they evolve from contrived secondary reinforcements, such as social praise, objects, activities, etc. There is a motivational interaction always present between behavior and communication acquisition, dependent on environment and the consequences within the environment. Natural environment increases the child's internal motivation, encouraging communicative responses when prompted rapidly by the presenters, and when encouraged to point to a keyboard.

RPT increases motivation relying on internal reinforcements and external reinforcements simultaneously in the beginning. It can be used during structured teaching sessions when not using RPM and in the context of the natural environment, such as eating, dressing, toileting, bathing, playing, etc. In RPT, the child naturally leads the trials with his or her own internal preference in a natural environment, and the therapist reinforces with the external reinforcement once the letters are pointed to.

Using both internal motivation (mand) and external motivation (tact of the reinforcement) at the same time increases the motivation to visually attend, track the letters, and point to the letters accurately. For example, a child is in the kitchen searching for a cookie. We present the keyboard for the child to point to "c-o-o-k-i-e." The child might initially need physical prompts to point. Once the child attempts to point, the cookie is given to the child.

The use of a laminated keyboard is important, because it allows for visual and motor reference for the child's information process of memory, organization of thoughts, attending to stimuli, and staying focused. The keyboard can also be used in adjunct with other methods of applied behavioral analysis, speech therapies, educational methods, etc. It reduces excitatory and obsessive behaviors, impeding learning and communicating that often occurs when using iPads and other assistive technology devices. It offers ease of use, the ability to have them hung up in multiple locations, and can travel with ease.

RPT begins with a preference assessment to identify the highest internal and external reinforcements of verbal operants. This is done to reinforce the use of the laminated alphabetic sheet choices, paired with the stimulus discriminate. It encourages the left and right hemispheres to connect attentively to what comes next. Furthermore, hemispheric connectivity fosters working memory and attending, with both the highest levels of reinforcement needed for success. The external reinforcement will fade on the child's internal reinforcement taking over the desire for mastery.

Operant behaviors are facilitated by eliciting a response from the child that includes, at a basic level, mands, echoics, tacts, and intraverbals. A mand is important to understand because it is the only operant to have an internal reinforcement for the child, while the other verbal operants are reinforced by secondary or external reinforcements. Remember to maintain important verbal behavior teaching procedures based on the operant variances; teach visual motor pointing success first; and initially start with high levels of reinforcement, paired with the most difficult task presented in a variable ratio schedule. Complete in small intervals initially, working up to larger intervals. Work in a natural environment preferably, intersperse the difficult tasks with those tasks already mastered, use prompting beneficial with the correct answers quickly, and then fade prompt quickly. Incorporating healthy cognitive statements for social-emotional growth, while stimulating information processing for memory is crucially important to remember.

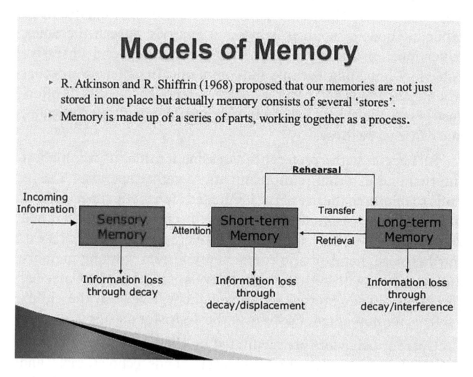

Models of Memory

- R. Atkinson and R. Shiffrin (1968) proposed that our memories are not just stored in one place but actually memory consists of several 'stores'.
- Memory is made up of a series of parts, working together as a process.

Operant	Antecedent/Stimuli	Behavior	Consequence
Mand: A request; to ask for something (a comMAND, deMAND, or counterMAND) due to deprivation or aversive stimulation.	1. Motivation of hunger. 2. Motivation of dry mouth from eating a cookie.	1. Says "cookie." 2. Says "water."	1. Gets the cookie. 2. Gets water or pushes away a cookie after offering.
Receptive Language: Following directions of others.	Give me the cookie.	The child gives the cookie.	Social/secondary reinforcer.
Imitation: Imitation is point-to-point correspondence between person and the child's behavior.	The teacher says, "Yum, eat the cookie."	Child imitates eating the cookie.	Social/secondary reinforcer.
Echoic: Repeating a word or sound that the speaker says.	Say "cookie."	Says "cookie."	Social/secondary reinforcer.
Tact: To label something (something you come in conTACT with).	Sees a cookie.	Says "cookie."	Social/secondary reinforcer.
Intraverbal: A fill in the blank or response to a question without the topic of conversation present.	We eat...	Says "cookie."	Social/secondary reinforcer.
Autoclitic: Modifies the functions of other verbal behaviors.	You like...	Says, "I like cookies."	Social/primary/ secondary reinforcer

— Adapted from B. F. Skinner, Theory of Verbal Operants

Motivating Children with Keyboard Matching and Fading

Applied behavioral analysis using a keyboard can increase various aspects of goal mastery by fostering the basis of how the brain and body work collectively together with impaired visual, auditory, tactile, kinesthetic, motor skills, and joint attention. Nonverbal and visual thinking skills are generally strengths for those with autism. Therefore, matching characteristics, both 2D and 3D, with a laminated alphabetic sheet is an optimal starting point. It helps children learn to associate items with the alphabet, develops independence in tasks, helps with generalization in expressive and receptive labeling, and is a precursor to many other aspects that require attention.

Keep in mind, vision dominances vary based on 2D versus 3D across the spectrum, making it erroneously appear that matching difficulties exist for some children with autism. Using simplistic visual approaches, like matching with an alphabetic symbolic language system, combined with 2D and 3D associations, covers all areas of brain functioning and will more likely lead to greater success. It also takes into account auditory and vocal skills, which are generally their greatest deficit, because we always sound out the letters, as they choose the correct letter out of a field of two, in early stages of use.

Practice sounding out the letters and asking, "What did I say?" with letters that sound fairly similar, such a "ba" and "da." While giving them the visual stimuli with options to point to the laminated alphabetic sheet out of a field of two, say "Dominic, 'ba' 'da.' Did I say 'ba' 'da' or 'ca' 'fa'? Practice with the letters simply next to each other, such as "d" and "e," or "j" and "k."

Teaching Receptive Language with a Keyboard

Supplement verbal information with pictures, visual schedules, gestures, visual examples, written directions, etc. Doing so while paired with a keyboard is imperative. Research indicates up to 75 percent of those diagnosed with autism also have a central auditory processing disorder. Considering the child's processing challenges and proceeding with quick timing to maintain attention and focus vastly improves results by pairing what is auditorily stated to encourage the child's receptive understanding. This increases the likelihood that the child is attending and following along visual and auditory dominant learning styles at the same time. Begin with simple, positively motivating words, avoiding complex verbal directions, information, and discussion. Immediately repeat the language prompt, while gesturally cueing the child to point at the beginning field of two, then expanding to larger fields is beneficial.

Teaching Expressive Language with a Keyboard

Because of working memory and word retrieval issues, children with autism oftentimes can't express the language in their minds even if they know the answer. Much of this is due to damage to their sensory motor neurons and motor processing. Utilizing a keyboard, simultaneously with visual supports and multiple-choice options, while beginning with a field of two, rectifies their presented deficits. For example, if we are teaching a child to ask for their favorite toy or edible, have a real-life picture of the "train" or "cookie," labeled with the words. Then, prompt the child to point to the letters, and reinforce the child with external reinforcement as he or she proceeds. Begin with visual supports that already exist in the natural environment, and have internal motivation paired with external reinforcement. This offers visual and working memory support for developing language and teaching. Expanding to sentences such as, "I want..." or "I like..." and adding the who, what, where, when, and why will occur over time with mastery.

Teaching Mands with a Keyboard

A mand is the foundation of all other verbal behavior. The child learns to ask for a need or want with or without the item in their vision or presence. What behaviorists call an "impure mand" results from an establishing operation and the stimulus discriminate being asked, "What do you want?" A "pure mand," results from the establishing operation being requested without being asked by someone. Mands also occur from peers, in sentences, for attention, and for information.

We chose a highly reinforcing need or want to be desired by the child, for example, a cookie. Present the cookie paired with a 2D-identical picture of the cookie with the identical letters "c-o-o-k-i-e," laminated to present as the 2D with a keyboard present. Start with a field of one, prompting the child to point to the letters. Once completed, provide the cookie for reinforcement. Multiple trials are necessary. Once one-letter acquisition is mastered, move to a field of two. Once a field of two is mastered, move to a field of four. Do NOT move to a field of three because you will train the child to select the middle and not discern. The long-term goal is to have the entire 26-letter alphabet keyboard chosen from.

A mand can also be taught with a keyboard transferring from an echoic. For example, if a child sees a cookie, but might not necessarily want the cookie, the presenter says, "cookie." The child can spell cookie independently on the keyboard, and then the teacher offers social or secondary reinforcement for spelling cookie. Mands are also taught as a tact transferring the mand when learning new words. If a child wants chips, but mands "cookie," we can redirect the child to juice saying, "This is juice," presenting the keyboard to type. If you know the child can type chip, then hold up the chip and also say, "What is this?" Present the chip with the keyboard and then reinforce after mastery.

It's important to reinforce the first tact with a generalized reinforcer, and transfer it to a pure mand. It is important to always transfer to the independent, so that the child does not become dependent on the prompts provided. It is also important to always provide the least- intrusive prompt, that is, if the child is successful with fill-ins, use those instead of echoic, as that is a less-intrusive prompt.

A mand should ultimately be taught with, "I want _____, please." Type this on a paper to laminate for the child to learn manding highly desired reinforcement for requesting an item. Repeat the steps above beginning with fields of one letter, two letters, four letters, to an entire field of 26. Highly preferred items can be listed for options, first paired with real photos and the letters. The pictures can quickly be faded, leaving only words with the child reading and typing mands, echoics, and tacts.

There are a few different types of response forms. Vocal, picture and object exchange, sign language, communication boards, as well as alternative and augmentative technology. I believe using the alphabet board is useful for both vocal and non-vocal children because humans all use letters and symbols to communicate and employ verbal operants. It encourages the left and right hemispheres to connect and pay attention to what comes next, fostering working memory. The use of a keyboard encourages functional behaviors, vocal production, engagement, and learning.

Teaching Echoics with a Keyboard

The word itself is descriptive. Echoing the word presented is an echoic. For example, the teacher says "cookie," and the child responds with "cookie." Echoics can be taught with the keyboard the same way the mands are taught; the only difference is there is no internal reinforcement or motivation. Say the letters out loud for the child as he or she points to the correct echoic. Reinforcement for an echoic, once pointing to the correct letters out of the fields, can be given if needed.

Teaching Tacts with a Keyboard

A tact means to label or name an item, action, or describe something within the environment of the child. If a child sees a cookie, but is not motivated or does not desire a cookie, labeling it "cookie" is a tact. The child can also tact, "brown cookie." The same procedural use of a keyboard applies here. Have the 2D-laminated picture of the item labeled with the spelling present with the 3D item. The child points to the field of one, then two, then four, and so forth. Once the child masters lower-level tacts of labeling objects, then move on to actions, parts, features, classes, and functions.

Teaching Intraverbal with a Keyboard

The interaction between verbal expressions, such as completing sentences, word associations, categorizing, and answering questions are intraverbals. For example, cookies are associated with pastries, while chocolate-chip cookies are categorized under types of cookies. Intraverbals allow conversations to occur derived from mands. Intraverbals can be transferred from fill-ins, tacts, or echoics by using a keyboard to facilitate exchanges between listener and speaker, teacher and child. The keyboard should be typed back and forth with the listener and speaker, teacher and child.

Training Stimulus Equivalence with a Keyboard

Matching to samples with a keyboard to achieve reflexivity, symmetry, and transitivity across the same stimulus class is a great way to quickly train working memory generalization to other members in an equivalent class, with long-term knowledge acquisition. Training an operant response this way, in the presence of a stimulus that is the member of the equivalence class, maximizes an applied behavioral analysis and educational program immensely.

All stimuli (any condition, event, or change in the physical world) in a class exerts control over a learner's behavior because a single common feature of the lesson or skill taught encourages the hemispheres of the brain to connect via associative processes that research has proven improves working memory.

A stimulus class is a group of stimuli with a common effect on a response class. Discriminative stimuli might have one or more common properties. For example, a red apple, a red toy, and a red pen, are all part of a stimulus class that represents red. Control by the commonality, "red," can be demonstrated when an individual correctly selects the red items from an array of differently colored items quickly; when the laminated alphabetic sheet field is provided, moving along quickly with the training stimulus equivalents by matching to various samples with letters on the board. That is, spelling "red" would be the single, common formal feature that evokes the same behavior (selecting the red item).

Children with autism struggle with identifying commonalities, as shown in these examples.

- To achieve reflexivity, the learner selects A given A, B given B, C given C, and so on. For example, a 2D-laminated picture of "cookie," labeled "c-o-o-k-i-e," with a 3D cookie for reinforcement once the child spells cookie out of a baseline field. The learner selects an identical stimulus as the reinforcer upon pointing.

- To mastery symmetry, the learner is taught to select B given A, and to select C given B. For example, given the picture of the cookie, say "cookie," with a field of various stimuli for options and the child points to the cookie on the keyboard. Following training, the learner is able to select A given B, and to select B given C. The learner is taught to select B given A, but as a result of training, can also select A given B.

- Finally, to achieve transitivity, the learner is taught to select B given A, and to select C given B. For example, given the spoken or modeled typed word, "cookie," the learner spells "cookie," and with the spoken word or modeled typed word, "cookie," the learner selects to a different looking type of cooking out of a field. Then with no further training, the learner spells the second type of "cookie." With no further training, the learner is able to select A given C, and to select C given A. The learner is taught to select B given A, and to select C given B, but as a result of the training, can also select A given C, and can select C given A.

CHAPTER 11

What Is an Exemplar Comprehensive Evidence-Based Program?

"There is no greater disability in society than the inability to see a person as more."

— ROBERT M. HENSEL

Examples of programs include the following.

1. antecedent-based intervention
2. cognitive behavioral intervention
3. differential reinforcement
4. discrete trial teaching
5. exercise
6. extinction
7. functional behavior assessment
8. functional communication training
9. modeling
10. naturalistic intervention
11. parent-implemented intervention

12. peer-mediated instruction and intervention
13. picture exchange communication system
14. pivotal response training
15. prompting
16. reinforcement
17. response interruption/redirection
18. scripting
19. self-management
20. social narratives
21. social skills training
22. structured play groups
23. task analysis
24. technology-aided instruction and intervention
25. time delay
26. video modeling
27. visual supports

Example of a Thorough Assessment and Intervention Plan

I. **Functional Behavioral Assessment and Intervention Plan**

II. **Identifying Information**
   a. Child Name: John Doe
   b. Date of Birth: 05/01/2007
   c. Present Address: 5555 Street Lane, City, CA 55555
   d. UCI #: 555555

e. Communication Mode: Keyboard with visuals and/or pointing to objects

f. Referring Service Coordinator: Jane Doe

g. Current Diagnoses: 299.00 Autism

h. Referral Date: 06/01/2017

i. Date of Report: 06/13/2017

j. Author's Name and Title: Jamie Juarez, MS, LMFT, PPSC, CWAC, PRTC

III. Referral Information

a. Source of Referral: Child was referred by service coordinator, Jane Doe, from the Regional Center of Orange County.

b. Referral Behaviors: Parents are concerned with John Doe's lack of communication skills, non-response to name or directives, lack of social skills, as well as aggression in the form of hitting, kicking and biting of others.

c. Current Reasons for Seeking Services from Hope, Inc.: Parents are seeking Behavior Modification including various evidence-based approaches: Applied Behavioral Analysis, Pivotal Response Training (PRT), Discrete Trial Training (DTT), Classical Conditioning, Antecedent Packages, Joint Attention Interventions, Peer Training Packages, Visual Schedules, Self-Management Interventions, Story-based Intervention Packages, Naturalistic Procedure Strategies, Video Modeling, and Functional Communication. All these techniques are evidenced based and utilized throughout the service hours.

IV. Description of Assessment Activities

a. Interviews: Conducted—6/13/2017 in school from 8:00–9:00am. Child's mother and child were present.

b. Record Reviews: Reviewed child's 2017 IEP provided by school district and reviewed child's psychological report dated 2011 provided by child's parent.

c. Direct Observation: Conducted—6/13/2017 in school from 9:00–11:00am and 6/14/2017 in child's home from 3:00– 4:00pm.

d. Other: Performed by clinician—DSM 5, GARS-2, CARS, CBDA, CBQ, and WebAblls.

DSM 5: symptoms reported by parent and observed by clinician meet the criteria for Mild Autism.

GARS-2: Standardized Scores: Stereotyped Behaviors: pending, Communication pending, Social Interaction pending, Total Autism Index: pending.

CARS: Pending.

WebAblls: Repertoires examined: Cooperation & Reinforcer Effectiveness, Visual Performance, Receptive Language, Motor Imitation, Vocal Imitation, Requests, Labeling, Intraverbals, Spontaneous Vocalizations, Syntax & Grammar, Play & Leisure, Social Interaction, Group Instruction, Follow Classroom Routines, Generalized Responding, Reading, Math, Writing, Spelling, Dressing, Eating, Grooming, Toileting, Gross Motor, Fine Motor. See report included for results.

V. Background Information

a. Child's Strengths

  i. Learning: John Doe really enjoys learning new information. He is attentive when new material is presented.

      ii. Receptive/Expressive Language: John Doe can answer basic questions through tacting responses on a letterboard.

      iii. Mobility: John Doe walks independently.

      iv. Self-Care: John Doe uses the restroom independently.

      v. Self-Direction: Will initiate music activities without prompting.

      vi. Independent Living: John Doe can take off clothing independently.

      vii. Economic Self-Sufficiency: N/A.

  b. Child's Deficits

      i. Learning: John Doe has difficulty retaining new material. There is some concern with mental capacity and working memory.

      ii. Receptive/Expressive Language: John Doe is delayed in expressive language. He does not verbally communicate and demonstrates some delays in receptive language.

      iii. Mobility: None.

      iv. Self-Care: John Doe does not brush teeth, groom, or dress self independently.

      v. Self-Direction: John Doe needs frequent direction from parents for non-preferred tasks.

      vi. Independent Living: John Doe cannot dress self-independently.

      vii. Economic Self-Sufficiency: N/A.

  c. Living Situation and Family History

      i. History of Living Arrangements: John Doe currently resides in home with both parents. He also lives with his two older brothers.

    ii. Cultural Issues: None.

    iii. Primary Language: The family's primary language is English.

    iv. Current Residential Situation: John Doe currently lives in the family home.

    v. Family Involvement: Parents are involved in services for John Doe. Parents attend all appointments with John Doe and are compliant with treatment recommendations.

d. School (Day Program) Placement and History

    i. History of School (or if adult, Day Program): John Doe has been receiving his education through his school district in Mild-Moderate Special Education.

    ii. Current School: John Doe currently attends first grade in a Mild-Moderate Special Education Class. Parents report he is doing well in school with the help of a 1:1 aide.

    iii. Hughes Bill Assessment or Behavioral Services at School (or Day Program): None.

e. Medical Conditions and Medications

    i. General Health: Client is in generally moderate health.

    ii. Open Medical Issues: Routine visits to primary care physician.

    iii. Seizure Activity: None.

    iv. Adaptive Physical Devices: None.

    v. Medications: None.

    vi. Relevant Medical History: None.

   f. Previous or Current Behavior Services

      i. Previous or Current Behavior Services & Vendors Involved: None.

     ii. Any Other Related Services: Client was receiving speech therapy through school district 1 hour per week.

   iii. Family/Caregivers' Impression of Effectiveness: Family did not feel the child was improving during speech therapy, since emphasis was on verbalizations rather than finding alternate ways to communicate.

VI. Functional Assessment

   a. Descriptive Phase

      i. Description of the Referred Target Behavior: Hitting others.

          1. Topography: Swinging arms and making physical contact with another, or swinging arms and hands with intent to make physical contact with another, even if the contact is avoided by the target person.

          2. Onset/Offset: An episode of hitting others occurs when the hand of the child makes contact with any body part of another, or attempt to make contact if target person avoids the actual physical contact, and ends when no attempt to make physical contact occurs for 3 minutes.

          3. Course of Behavior: When client gets upset, he will swing his arm with intent to make contact to another person's body. The behavior ends when no attempt to hit others occurs for at least 3 minutes. This occurs across environments (in home, clinic, and school settings).

4. Baseline Data: The frequency for hitting others occurs between 3 and 5 times in a given 30-minute period.

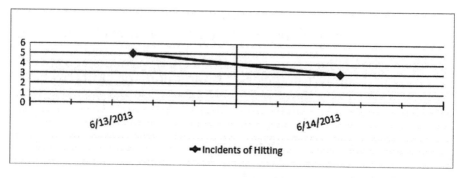

Incidents of Hitting

ii. History

1. Onset: Family reports the hitting behavior started when the client was 3 years old.

2. Recent Changes in Behavior: Parents report no recent changes in behavior.

3. Coincidental Environmental Changes: Family could not identify any new environmental changes that might impact behavior.

iii. Antecedents

1. Setting Events

a. Behavior Most Likely to Occur When:

☒ A request to answer question during conversation initiation by another.

☒ A behavioral request to do or to stop.

☒ Child in setting with other peers such as recess, play time, etc.

☒ Structure/environmental changes.

☒ Consequence imposed: Nonpreferred item.

☐ Clinician occupied/unavailable.

☐ Other

b. Behavior Least Likely to Occur When:

☐ A request to answer question during conversation initiation by another.

☐ A behavioral request to do or to stop.

☐ Child in setting with other peers such as recess, play time, etc.

☐ Structure/environmental changes.

☐ Consequence imposed: Nonpreferred item.

☒ Clinician occupied/unavailable.

☒ Other: Client allowed access to preferred item, or activity.

2. Trigger Events

a. Location: Clinic, Home, School and Community

b. Persons: Parents, siblings, caregivers, and staff

c. Time: AM & PM

d. Activities/Events: Occurs across all work, academic, and leisure activities.

3. Consequences

a. Family/Caregivers' Behavior: Gives in to child's demands and allows escape from task, or gives desired activity.

b. Others' Behavior: siblings and peers move away from client when hitting behavior occurs.

c. Subsequent Child Behavior: Behavior will initially decrease if he gets what he wants, or if there is no one there to hit, but if not given what he wants, he will follow the target person and continue attempted hitting.

iv. Interpretation Phase

1. Analysis of Meaning/Hypothesis: Hitting behaviors were hypothesized to be controlled by the following.

   a. Gaining access to tangible items.

   b. Escape and avoiding demands or non-preferred tasks.

v. Verification Phase

1. Experimentally Manipulated Variables or

2. Intervention Implemented

   To verify the function of hitting behaviors, we completed a brief functional behavioral analysis (FBA).

   Our hypothesis was that hitting behaviors was related to the functions: ***gain access and escape.***

   We used 5-minute intervals to assess hitting behavior in a variety of conditions: play, tangible, demand, and attention.

VII. Mediator Analysis

a. Analysis of Mediators: Both parents participated in the FBA. Parents are willing to comply with treatment recommendations. After discussing the functions of the behavior, the family clearly understands how the current consequences are inadvertently reinforcing the hitting behavior. It was discussed with the family that all family members will need to be consistent in not giving in to all the wants and needs of the client that might evoke hitting.

VIII. Environmental/Ecological Analysis

a. Physical Environment: The child's physical environment currently meets his needs.

b. Programmatic Environment: His environment is currently unstructured, allowing him access to do and gain whatever he wants. His environment will need to become more structured. No visual aides are available in the home and will be needed. Preferred items will need to be limited so that they can be saved for reinforcement items.

c. Social/Interpersonal Environment: The client currently has access to social interactions with peers and siblings in the home, school, and community.

d. Reinforcer Survey

   i. Method of Analysis: Preference Assessment

   ii. List Potential Reinforcers: Snickers candy, oranges, putty, grapes, yogurt, iPad, trains

   iii. Limited Reinforcers: N/A

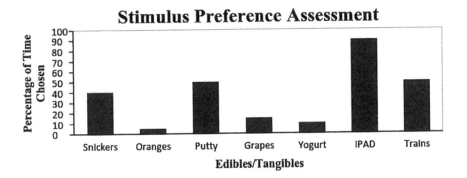

IX. Ultimate and Instrumental Goals

a. Ultimate Goal # 1: John Doe will communicate his basic wants and needs across different settings, people, and activities, 80 percent of the time, without engaging in hitting others, for four consecutive weeks.

b. Instrumental Goals

#1 Request (Indicating Specific Items/Activities Desired) Operational Definition of John Doe's behavior targeted: JOHN DOE will be able to specifically indicate 5 items or 5 activities, which he wants by pointing to the item, or by manding and/or tacting the item on a keyboard.

Baseline: As of June 2017, JOHN DOE is unable to specifically indicate 5 items or 5 activities that he wants by pointing to, manding or tacting the item on a keyboard.

Short-Term Benchmarks

By September 2017, JOHN DOE will indicate 1 preferred item by either pointing to a picture of the item, or by tacting on a keyboard to request the item with prompting 4 of 10 opportunities.

By December 2017, JOHN DOE will indicate 3 preferred items by either pointing to a picture of the items, or by tacting on a keyboard to request the items with prompting 8 of 10 opportunities.

By March 2017, JOHN DOE will indicate 5 preferred items by either pointing to a picture of the item, or by tacting on a keyboard to request the items without a prompt, 4 of 10 opportunities.

By June 2017, JOHN DOE will indicate 5 preferred items by either pointing to a picture or the items, or by tacting on a keyboard to request the items, without a prompt, 8 of 10 opportunities.

2 Vocal Response (as it pertains to noncompliance)

Operational definition of JOHN DOE's behavior targeted: JOHN DOE will learn to respond to a greeting such as hi by saying, "Hi" or typing, "Hi," while making eye contact.

Baseline: As of June 2017, JOHN DOE does not make eye contact when greeted by others, nor does he respond.

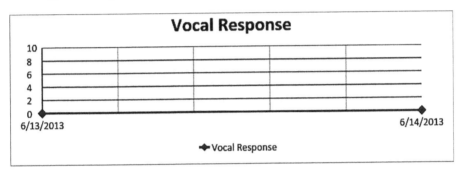

Short-Term Benchmarks

By September 2017, JOHN DOE will respond to a greeting, such as, "Hi," typing, "Hi," with eye contact, with prompting 4 of 10 opportunities.

By December 2017, JOHN DOE will respond to a greeting, such as, "Hi," typing, "Hi," with eye contact, with prompting 8 of 10 opportunities.

By March 2017, JOHN DOE will respond to a greeting, such as, "Hi," typing, "Hi," with eye contact, and by verbalizing "hi," without a prompt, 4 of 10 opportunities.

By June 2017, JOHN DOE will respond to a greeting, such as, "Hi," typing, "Hi," with eye contact and by verbalizing "Hi," without a prompt, 8 of 10 opportunities.

A. Ultimate Goal # 2: John Doe will identify emotions of self and others, and learn to express emotions appropriately on a keyboard across different settings, people, and activities 80 percent of the time, without engaging in hitting others, for four consecutive weeks.

B. Instrumental Goals

#1 Labeling Emotions

Operational definition of JOHN DOE's behavior targeted: JOHN DOE will learn to identify emotions of self and others on a keyboard.

Baseline: As of June 2017, JOHN DOE does not identify any emotions.

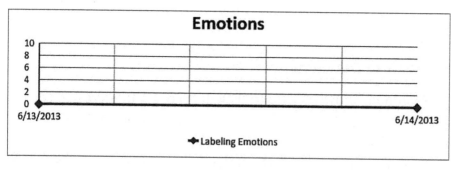

Short-Term Benchmarks

By September 2017, JOHN DOE will learn to identify 2 emotions on a keyboard, when prompted, 8 of 10 opportunities.

By December 2017, JOHN DOE will learn to identify 3 emotions on a keyboard, without prompting, 4 of 10 opportunities.

By March 2017, JOHN DOE will learn to identify 4 emotions on a keyboard, without prompting, 6 of 10 opportunities.

By June 2017, JOHN DOE will learn to identify 5 emotions, without prompting, 8 of 10 opportunities.

2 Emotional Expression

Operational definition of JOHN DOE's behavior targeted: JOHN DOE will learn to use emotions on a keyboard in social communication to express himself rather than engaging in aggressive behaviors.

Baseline: As of June 2017, JOHN DOE does not verbally express emotions in social conversation or times of frustration.

Short-Term Benchmarks

By September 2017, JOHN DOE will express emotions in conversation on a keyboard as they pertain to his current feelings and/or recent experiences with prompting 4 of 10 opportunities.

By December 2017, JOHN DOE will express emotions in conversation on a keyboard as they pertain to his current feelings and/or recent experiences with prompting 8 of 10 opportunities.

By March 2017, JOHN DOE will express emotions in conversation on a keyboard as they pertain to his current feelings and/or recent experiences without prompting 4 of 10 opportunities.

By June 2017, JOHN DOE will express emotions in conversation on a keyboard as they pertain to his current feelings and/or recent experiences without prompting 8 of 10 opportunities.

A. **Ultimate Goal # 3:** John Doe will initiate and complete his daily routine across different settings and people 80 percent of the time, without engaging in hitting behavior for four consecutive weeks.

B. **Instrumental Goal**

1 Self-Help Skills

Operational definition of JOHN DOE's behavior targeted: JOHN DOE will initiate and complete his daily routine with the help of a visual schedule/checklist/self-management intervention without being prompted. Daily routine will include brush teeth, shower, and dress self independently.

Baseline: As of June 2017, JOHN DOE does not have a visual schedule. He needs constant prompting in order to complete the activities in his daily routine.

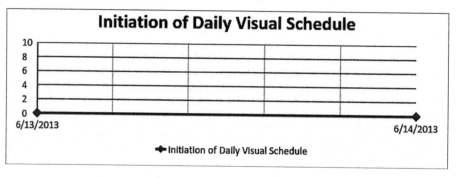

Short-Term Benchmarks

By September 2017, JOHN DOE will learn to initiate (even if all items are not completed) tasks on a visual schedule, with use of a keyboard with prompting for 4 of 10 opportunities.

By December 2017, JOHN DOE will learn to initiate and attempt to complete tasks on a visual schedule with use of a keyboard with prompting for 8 of 10 opportunities.

By March 2017, JOHN DOE will initiate and complete all tasks on a visual schedule with use of a keyboard without prompting for 4 of 10 opportunities.

By June 2017, JOHN DOE will learn to initiate and complete all tasks on a visual schedule with use of a keyboard without prompting for 8 of 10 opportunities.

A. **Ultimate Goal # 4:** John Doe will wait for his turn and follow directions across different settings, people, and activities, 80 percent of the time, without engaging in hitting others, for four consecutive weeks.

B. **Instrumental Goals**

1 Waiting

Operational Definition of JOHN DOE's behavior targeted: JOHN DOE will wait for a turn typing, "I can wait," with use of a keyboard, item, or activity for up to 2 minutes when prompted.

Baseline: As of June 2017, JOHN DOE is unable to wait for a preferred item or activity, without being physically prompted by a parent or therapist.

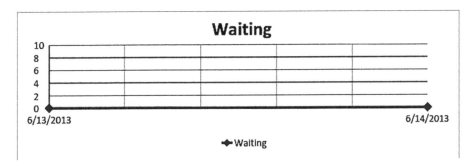

Short-Term Benchmarks

By September 2017, JOHN DOE will wait for a preferred item or activity typing, "I can wait," with use of a keyboard for at least 30 seconds when prompted 4 of 10 opportunities.

By December 2017, JOHN DOE will wait for a preferred item or activity typing, "I can wait," with use of a keyboard for at least 30 seconds, when prompted 8 of 10 opportunities.

By March 2017, JOHN DOE will wait for a preferred item or activity typing, "I can wait," with use of a keyboard for at least 1 minute, without prompting 4 of 10 opportunities.

By June 2017, JOHN DOE will wait for a preferred item or activity typing, "I can wait," with use of a keyboard for at least 2 minutes, without prompting 8 of 10 opportunities.

2 Compliance with Non-Preferred Directives in a Timely Manner

Operational Definition of JOHN DOE's behavior targeted: JOHN DOE will learn to comply within a reasonable time period by parents, therapists, and other authority figures without prompting.

Baseline: As of June 2017, JOHN DOE is unable to comply within a reasonable time period with parents, therapists, and other authority figures without prompting.

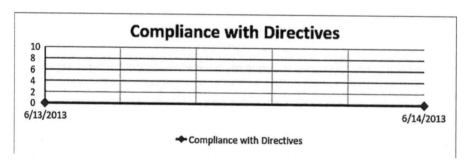

Short-Term Benchmarks

By September 2017, JOHN DOE will comply within 40 seconds, when prompted, 4 out of 10 opportunities.

By December 2017, JOHN DOE will comply within 40 seconds, when prompted, 8 out of 10 opportunities.

By March 2017, JOHN DOE will comply within 40 seconds, without prompting, 4 out of 10 opportunities.

By June 2017, JOHN DOE will comply within 40 seconds, without prompting, 8 out of 10 opportunities.

A. **Ultimate Goal # 5:** John Doe will play with peers appropriately across different settings, people, and activities, 80 percent of the time, without engaging in hitting others, for four consecutive weeks.

B. **Instrumental Goal**

1 Interactive Play

Operational definition of JOHN DOE's behavior targeted: JOHN DOE will independently engage in appropriate play with peers without engaging in hitting behavior.

Baseline: As of June 2017, JOHN DOE is unable to engage in play with peers.

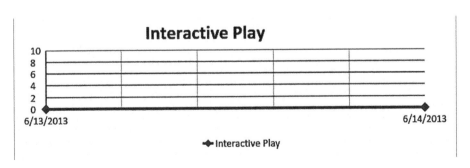

155

Short-Term Benchmarks

By September 2017, JOHN DOE will engage in appropriate play with peers, when prompted, 4 out of 10 opportunities.

By December 2017, JOHN DOE will engage in appropriate play with peers, when prompted, 8 out of 10 opportunities.

By March 2017, JOHN DOE will engage in appropriate play with peers, without prompting, 4 out of 10 opportunities.

By June 2017, JOHN DOE will engage in appropriate play with peers, without prompting, 8 out of 10 opportunities.

Family/Caregiver(s) Training and Monitoring

A. **Ultimate Parent Goal:** JOHN DOE's parents will participate in his intervention and utilize appropriate techniques correctly, 80 percent of the time across all settings and behaviors, for four consecutive weeks.

B. **Instrumental Parent Goals**

1 Functional Communication

Operational definition: JOHN DOE's parent will work with him to be able to specifically indicate 5 items or 5 activities that he wants by pointing to the item, or by manding and/or tacting the item.

Baseline: As of June 2017, JOHN DOE'S parents have no previous training in behavioral intervention and do not work with him on tacting skills.

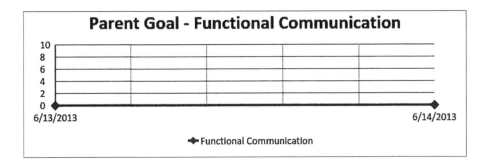

Short-Term Benchmarks

By September 2017, JOHN DOE's parents will have him indicate 1 preferred item by either pointing to a picture of the item, or by tacting to request the item with prompting 4 of 10 opportunities.

By December 2017, JOHN DOE's parents will have him indicate 3 preferred items by either pointing to a picture of the items, or by tacting to request the items with prompting 8 of 10 opportunities.

By March 2017, JOHN DOE's parents will have him indicate 5 preferred items by either pointing to a picture of the item, or by tacting to request the items without a prompt, 4 of 10 opportunities.

By June 2017, JOHN DOE's parents will have him indicate 5 preferred items by either pointing to a picture or the items, or by tacting to request the items, without a prompt, 8 of 10 opportunities.

2 Self-Help Skills—Daily Visual Schedule

Operational Definition: JOHN DOE's parents will encourage him to initiate and complete his daily routine with the help of a visual schedule/checklist/self-management intervention without being prompted. Daily routine will include brush teeth, shower, and dress self independently.

Baseline: As of June 2017, JOHN DOE'S parents have no previous training in behavioral intervention and do not encourage him to complete his daily schedule.

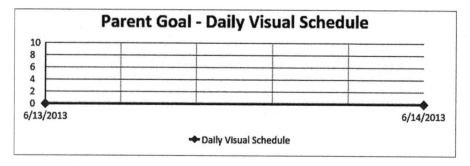

Short-Term Benchmarks

By September 2017, JOHN DOE's parents will encourage him to initiate (even if all items are not completed) tasks on a visual schedule with a keyboard without prompting for 4 of 10 opportunities.

By December 2017, JOHN DOE's parents will encourage him to initiate and attempt to complete tasks on a visual schedule with a keyboard with prompting for 8 of 10 opportunities.

By March 2017, JOHN DOE's parents will encourage him to initiate and complete all tasks on a visual schedule with a keyboard without prompting for 4 of 10 opportunities.

By June 2017, JOHN DOE's parents will encourage him to initiate and complete all tasks on a visual schedule with a keyboard without prompting for 8 of 10 opportunities.

3 Compliance

Operational definition: JOHN DOE's parents will encourage him to comply with non-preferred directives within a reasonable time figures without prompting.

Baseline: As of June 2017, JOHN DOE'S parents have no previous training in behavioral intervention and do not encourage him to comply with directives consistently.

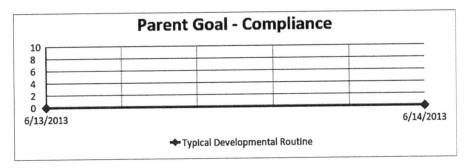

Short-Term Benchmarks

By September 2017, JOHN DOE's parents will encourage him to comply with non-preferred directives, within forty seconds, when prompted, 4 out of 10 opportunities.

By December 2017, JOHN DOE's parents will encourage him to comply with non-preferred directives, within forty seconds, when prompted, 8 out of 10 opportunities.

By March 2017, JOHN DOE's parents will encourage him to comply with non-preferred directives, within forty seconds, without prompting, 4 out of 10 opportunities.

By June 2017, JOHN DOE's parents will encourage him to comply with non-preferred directives, within forty seconds, without prompting, 8 out of 10 opportunities.

Parent Training: Rapid Prompting Training's Your Child Can Type

A. Knowledge of behavior analytic principles: We provide training for parents on behavioral intervention techniques as part of JOHN DOE's authorized hours. We require JOHN DOE's parents to continuously be part of their child's therapy at a rate of 50 percent direct participation. Every child's parent will ultimately be able to independently implement a behavioral program aimed to promote positive social behaviors and reduce or ameliorate behaviors that interfere with the child's adaptive skills and social interaction.

The following areas shall be covered with the parents during the child's sessions to achieve this goal.

1. Functional communication. Child's parents will learn to verbally communicate, exchange a PECS icon, or use an augmentative device. This results in the ability to have socially appropriate behaviors and reduce behavioral frustrations because of the inability to communicate.

2. Spontaneous language/communication in order to promote socialization skills and enhance generalization.

3. Generalization that is planned and measured as a variable with respect to the child's mastery of concepts. Each child rotates to different centers depending on the activity.

4. Typical developmental routines (preparing for transitions, raising hand, following group instructions), as well as functional activities that occur within those routines.

5. Self-help skills that are designed to relate to daily routines and home environment (using the bathroom, cleaning up after oneself, and dressing oneself).

6. Play skill lessons that are designed to bridge communication and social skill objectives that will lead to more independence.

7. Language concepts and early academia preparing a child to continue communicating and socializing in his/her learning environments. Nonverbal children need to know their alphabet to socialize and communicate and to reduce frustrating behaviors by means of a Go Talk, Fusion, and other augmentative communication devices.

8. Behavior plans work collaboratively with the parents to address problematic behaviors, so as to not interfere with a child's learning, or present a danger to the child or to others.

9. Provide parenting skills and strategies to parents so they can help their children when professional support is unavailable.

B. Application of behavior analytic principles: The parents will be expected to continue applying behavioral procedures taught to them in the child's home and community environment outside of direct therapy sessions. Parents will be required to document and provide us with their own supportive data. Data sheets for tracking trials, scatter plots, and fidelity forms will be provided to the parents. Data will be reviewed during supervision sessions.

a. Method of teaching: There are many designs for behavior programs. Treatment procedures can be either accelerative (those designed to increase the frequency or duration of a target behavior), decelerative (those designed to decrease the frequency or duration of a target behavior), or complex (those having characteristics of both accelerative and decelerative programs).

- Discrete Trial Training: Discrete trial training (DTT) is a component of most ABA programs for children with developmental delays. There is strong evidence that these techniques can produce rapid gains. DTT consists of a series of repeated lessons or broken-down trials taught 1:1. For younger children, we often begin with a series of brief, simple trials that build on skills and help to increase attention span, focus, and compliance. DTT encourages motivation by rewarding certain behaviors with external reinforcements, such as praise, edibles, toys, extra time to play, and so forth. Random rotating with error stimulates brain function and memory. Tell-ask procedures are important for all learning because it addresses working memory.

- Pivotal Response Training: Pivotal response training (PRT) is used to teach behaviors that are central to broad areas of functioning. Rather than target specific behaviors one at a time, PRT focuses on pivotal behaviors that can lead to improvements in other areas of behavior. A strength of pivotal response training is enhanced motivation. Children with developmental delays typically lack the motivation to learn new tasks and participate in their social environment, which might be observed as temper tantrums, crying, fidgeting, staring, noncompliance, inattention, or lethargy. PRT targets motivation through internal reinforcements by encouraging the child to respond to increasing expectations related to communication and socialization. Methods such as turn-taking, child choice, modeling, shaping, and direct reinforcement are emphasized. This method is more child-led, in that the child plays a central role in determining what activities and objects will be used for reinforcement during a PRT session.

- Pivotal behaviors should be assessed. Behaviors that are considered pivotal and highly influential should be addressed first. Pivotal behaviors targeted must include motivation and attention.

- Pivotal behaviors should also include teaching a child how to acquire the ability to mand, tact, echo, and utilize intraverbal communication.

- To teach fluency-based instruction, you must also assess the child's strengths based on standard knowledge of learning modalities by use of a keyboard and emerging RPT: visual, auditory, tactile, kinesthetic, and olfactory. When teaching fluency-based instruction, it is imperative that the child attend through their dominant learning modalities. Make sure the child has scanned the answer choices before choosing, or the response is void. To ensure they scan choices prior to allowing them to choose the answer, gently restrain their hands before giving them the opportunity to choose.

- Accelerative programs involve positive programming, shaping, and chaining.

   i. Positive programming is teaching individual new skills through the use of reinforcing consequences. Activities of daily living, functional communication, and social skills training are all examples of positive programming.

   ii. Shaping teaches gradual approximations of a target behavior. For example, teaching someone to be able to get his or her arm into the sleeve when learning to put on a shirt.

   iii. Chaining involves teaching the whole sequence of steps to a task. For example, teaching each step of the sequence required to put on a shirt.

- Decelerative programs involve several different reinforcement procedures.

    i. Differential reinforcement of incompatible behaviors (DRI) involves reinforcing behaviors that are different from, or incompatible with, the target behavior. For example, keeping one's hands in one's lap is incompatible with hitting oneself.

    ii. Differential reinforcement of other behaviors (DRO) reinforces any behavior other than the target behavior for a specific interval of time. For example, reinforcers are given for a specific time interval during which physical aggression is not exhibited.

    iii. Differential reinforcement of low rates of behavior (DRL) reinforces behaviors if a specified period of time has elapsed since the behavior last occurred, or if there have been only a specified number of episodes during a particular interval. For example, if the behavior is yelling, the client is rewarded for each 15-minute interval that passes since yelling occurred, or for each interval in which yelling occurs below a certain rate.

- There are two types of overcorrection procedures, restitutional and positive practice.

    i. Restitutional overcorrection requires that a person return the environment to a state better than before his or her behavioral episode.

    ii. Positive practice overcorrection requires repeated practice of an appropriate behavior.

    iii. Stimulus change is a sudden introduction of an unrelated stimulus that results in a temporary reduction of the behavior. For example, clapping once, loudly, while a client is yelling will redirect his or her attention and temporarily stop the yelling.

iv. Stimulus satiation allows the person unrestricted access to the reinforcer of the behavior.

v. Time-out procedures are either nonseclusionary or exclusionary. Nonseclusionary time-out involves withdrawing attention from a person while remaining in his or her presence. Exclusionary time-out involves removing the person from the environment following behavior episode.

- Complex behavior programs involve contracting, stimulus control, and token economies.

  i. Contracting is a written agreement between the client and another person.

  ii. Stimulus control brings the target behavior under the control of a specific stimulus or set of conditions. Behaviors are brought under control by reinforcing the target behavior at the time and location where the behavior should naturally or acceptably occur. For example, urinating in the bathroom rather than in public.

  iii. Token economies use reinforcers that the client earns and which can be traded later for something of value to the client. For example, poker chips awarded for positive behaviors can be traded for a trip to the movies.

2. Family/Caregiver(s) Involvement: We provide training for parents weekly on behavioral intervention techniques employed as part of their child's authorized hours. We also require parents to continuously be part of their child's

therapy, overlapping on session weekly. Parents are required to implement trials, provide positive reinforcement, track data, discover the antecedents to their behaviors, and apply the proper consequence accordingly. Equally incorporated into the patient's program is typical peer exposure, especially if they have a sibling or related family member close in age. We have many established relationships with local private schools with typical children grades, preschool to high school, who volunteer at our clinic in the afternoon to interact with our patients diagnosed with autism as part of their community service hours. Parents are required to sign consent for this aspect of natural environment, modeled behavior exposure.

3. Monitoring Family/Caregiver(s) Progress: Direct observation and parent data will be used to monitor the progress of the family in utilizing behavioral interventions.

XV. Intervention Strategies

A. **Ecological Strategies:** Strategies to improve our child's environments within his or her individualized households, interactions, and within the community linked to the functional assessment must occur. Arranging the environment with reinforcement based on stimulus preferences, removal of self-stimulatory provocation, and training appropriate individuals who interact with the child, are all examples of the ecological strategies employed. Further manipulations of therapeutic methods are always in consideration of the ecological influences.

B. Teaching Replacement Behaviors

1. Rationale/Logic: Replacement behaviors to either increase or decrease the behaviors based on our

FBA will occur. For example, a child will be taught to request desired items during structured time, and NET appropriately and with the same function (if achievable), instead of employing inappropriate requesting behaviors. The same will occur for attention, escape, and self-stimulatory behaviors based on the antecedent and consequence format indicated on the FA.

2. Structured Situation: Goals are structured formally appropriate according to their logical flow on the FA, while teaching functionally equivalent replacement behavior (FERB). This will assist the 1:1 time management organization to increase the functional skills taught. The child's goals are promoted during structured settings based on the evidence-based methodologies utilized. This will occur at table time discrete trials in a play-based, natural environment during pivotal response training. There will be parent participation, modeling of evidence-based therapy methods, strategies to promote compliance within the prompt hierarchy, delivery of reinforcements, and clear instruction during structured settings.

3. Unstructured Situation: Goals are structured formally, appropriate according to their logical flow on the FA and while teaching FERB, using pivotal response training in a child-led, natural environment. This will assist the 1:1 time management organization to increase the functional skills taught within unstructured time when the environment is child-led and a natural setting. The child's goals are promoted in unstructured settings based on the evidence-based methodologies utilized, more specifically incidental teaching and pivotal response training. This will

occur during play-based therapy, in a natural environment during pivotal response training, or incidental teaching procedures. There will be parent participation, modeling of evidence-based therapy methods, strategies to promote compliance within the prompt hierarchy, delivery of reinforcements, and clear instruction in unstructured settings.

C. **Focused Intervention Strategies:** Intervention strategies are employed to produce the rapid acquisition of skills for each targeted goal and behavior. Examples include positive reinforcement and negative reinforcement, both contingent/time-based and non-contingent (fixed and interval), DRI, DRO, DRA, and antecedent manipulations derived from the FA.

D. **Reactive Strategies:** Operational definitions of treatment procedures for each target behavior are either increasing (the FERB) or decreasing (maladaptive behaviors) based on the FBA, which are taught for each targeted behavior. Techniques to prevent escalation are implemented in line with the functions of behavior.

E. **Generalization and Maintenance Plan**

1. Generalization/Maintenance: Emphasis is given to teaching similar skills and FERBs in various settings with multiple people. Once generalization is met by mastery of taught skills in multiple environments with multiple people, fading of support will occur.

2. Thinning Reinforcement Schedule: Initial reinforcement of correct responses occur on higher reinforcement frequencies moving toward intermittent schedules of reinforcement once toleration and skill progression occurs.

3. Transition to Natural Mediators: Parent and caretaker participation is imperative to fading out therapists and promoting generalization to natural mediators. Significant progress on goals to fade out dependency and translating skills acquisition to the natural environment is tracked individually.

F. **Relapse Prevention:** Assurance of mastery and generalization prior to fading, maintenance of natural mediators, and interspersed promotion of those previously mastered skills.

G. **Data Collection**

1. Methods: The frequency and/or duration of specified behaviors indicated are tracked over trials. Parents are required to collect data when sessions are not under therapist control. The ABC data is also tracked according to the FBA findings and scatter plotted/ charted to track growth progression.

2. Monitoring

   a. Target Behavior(s) of Concern: Data tracking and charting accordingly ensures monitoring of the specified target behaviors. Tracking on specific interventions and impact paired with percentage of acquisition are monitored as well.

   b. Replacement Behavior: Data tracking and charting accordingly ensures monitoring of the specified target behaviors. Tracking on specific interventions and impact paired with percentage of acquisition are monitored as well on the FERBs.

3. Procedural Reliability: The reliability of therapeutic interventions is ensured by collecting data on goal progression matched to the therapeutic model

employed. Strategies and interventions are taught and then tracked by both the therapist and parents/caregiver.

XI. Summary and Recommendations

A. General Summary and Statement of Need: Assessment findings are summarized with the totality of data collection, domain deficit determination, FBA/FAA, operationally defined treatment goals with baselines and benchmarks, transition requirements, and need based on evidence-based protocols and service hours are provided. Based on this assessment, John Doe displays delays in communication, socialization, self-help, and compliance without aggressive behaviors. The data determined that the function of the hitting behavior was access to tangibles and escape and avoidance of work. Behavioral intervention and parent training will help in decreasing the frequency of maladaptive behaviors as well as increasing appropriate functionally equivalent behaviors and positive programming to improve self-help, social, and adaptive skills deficits.

B. Recommended Services

	Per Month	Per Reporting Period
Monthly Direct 1:1 Services	40	120
Monthly Supervision	4	12

XII. Signatures

_____

Parent/Guardian   Date

_____

Jamie Juarez Melillo, MS, LMFT, PPSC, CWAC, PRTC   Date

Data Summary w/ Interventions Example

| Child Name | Provider Name |

Monday	Time	Tuesday	Time	Wednesday	Time
Benchmarks/ Beh. Goals		Benchmarks/ Beh. Goals		Benchmarks/ Beh. Goals	
Requests Comm/Mand		Requests Comm/Mand		Requests Comm/Mand	
Adaptive Skills		Adaptive Skills		Adaptive Skills	
Receptive Language		Receptive Language		Receptive Language	
Receptive Labels		Receptive Labels		Receptive Labels	
Vocal Initiation		Vocal Initiation		Vocal Initiation	
Non-Vocal Initiation		Non-Vocal Initiation		Non-Vocal Initiation	
Soc./Emotional Tantrums		Soc./Emotional Tantrums		Soc./Emotional Tantrums	
Self-Help Skills		Self-Help Skills		Self-Help Skills	
Visual Performance		Visual Performance		Visual Performance	
Imitations		Imitations		Imitations	
Social Interaction		Social Interaction		Social Interaction	
Fine Motor		Fine Motor		Fine Motor	
Gross Motor		Gross Motor		Gross Motor	
Interactive Play		Interactive Play		Interactive Play	
Novel Toy Exposure		Novel Toy Exposure		Novel Toy Exposure	

Data Summary w/ Interventions Example

1:1 Aide Name   For the Week of: Year

Thursday	_____ Time	Friday	_____ Time	Saturday	_____ Time
Benchmarks/ Beh. Goals		Benchmarks/ Beh. Goals		Benchmarks/ Beh. Goals	
Requests Comm/Mand		Requests Comm/Mand		Requests Comm/Mand	
Adaptive Skills		Adaptive Skills		Adaptive Skills	
Receptive Language		Receptive Language		Receptive Language	
Receptive Labels		Receptive Labels		Receptive Labels	
Vocal Initiation		Vocal Initiation		Vocal Initiation	
Non-Vocal Initiation		Non-Vocal Initiation		Non-Vocal Initiation	
Soc./Emotional Tantrums		Soc./Emotional Tantrums		Soc./Emotional Tantrums	
Self-Help Skills		Self-Help Skills		Self-Help Skills	
Visual Performance		Visual Performance		Visual Performance	
Imitations		Imitations		Imitations	
Social Interaction		Social Interaction		Social Interaction	
Fine Motor		Fine Motor		Fine Motor	
Gross Motor		Gross Motor		Gross Motor	
Interactive Play		Interactive Play		Interactive Play	
Novel Toy Exposure		Novel Toy Exposure		Novel Toy Exposure	

Techniques	Techniques	Techniques	Techniques	Techniques
DTT (External Rein)	DTT (External Rein)	DTT (External Rein)	DTT (External Rein)	DTT (External Rein)
PRT (Internal Rein)	PRT (Internal Rein)	PRT (Internal Rein)	PRT (Internal Rein)	PRT (Internal Rein)
RPT (Keyboard)	RPT (Keyboard)	RPT (Keyboard)	RPT (Keyboard)	RPT (Keyboard)
Classical Conditioning	Classical Conditioning	Classical Conditioning	Classical Conditioning	Classical Conditioning
Cognitive Behavioral	Cognitive Behavioral	Cognitive Behavioral	Cognitive Behavioral	Cognitive Behavioral
Functional Comm.	Functional Comm.	Functional Comm.	Functional Comm.	Functional Comm.
Video Modeling	Video Modeling	Video Modeling	Video Modeling	Video Modeling
Beh. ABC's	Beh. ABC's	Beh. ABC's	Beh. ABC's	Beh. ABC's
			Date Treatment Plan Updated	Date Uploaded in Google Drives:
Teacher Signature	1:1 Aide Signature	Parent Signature	_____	_____

A Reference Guide to Common Behavioral Terminology

ABA Terms	Definition
ABC Recording	A direct observation that can be used to collect information occurring within a student's environment by looking at the antecedent, behavior, and consequence.
Accelerative Program	Behavioral plan designed to increase the frequency or duration of a target behavior.
Acquisition Task	A skill that is in the process of being taught.
Antecedent	The event(s), action(s), or circumstance(s) that occur immediately before a behavior.
Antecedent Intervention	An intervention designed to alter the environment before a behavior occurs, for example, priming, visuals, etc.
Applied Behavioral Analysis (ABA)	Behavioral analysis that focuses on the principles that explain how learning takes place.
Baseline	The current level that a behavior occurs at before intervention.
Behavior	An observable and measurable action of a living thing.
Behavior Intervention Plan	Developed to guide parents, teachers, and other professionals on how to decrease inappropriate behaviors and to teach, or increase, replacement behaviors in all settings.
Behavioral Momentum	A metaphor to describe a rate of responding and its resistance to change following an alteration in reinforcement conditions.

ABA Terms	Definition
Benchmark	The short-term goals listed in the treatment plan that have been broken down quarterly.
Chaining	Teaching the whole sequence of steps to a task by adding on more steps until the entire task.
Classical Conditioning	The conditioned stimulus (sound of a bell) is paired with the unconditioned stimulus (sight of food) until the conditioned stimulus alone is sufficient to elicit a response (salivation in dog when bell rings).
Cognitive Behavioral Therapy	Therapy that focuses on understanding how events and experiences are interpreted. Focuses on identifying and changing the distortions or deficits that occur in cognitive processing.
Compulsions	Deliberate repetitive behaviors that follow specific rules, such as pertaining to cleaning, checking, or counting.
Consequence	The action(s) or response(s) that immediately follow the behavior.
Consequence Intervention	Strategies that address the stimuli that follow a behavior.
Contingency	Refers to dependent and/or temporal relations between operant behavior and its controlling variables.
Continuous Reinforcement	Reward given after each response.
Contract Writing	A written agreement between the client and another person.
Crisis Prevention Intervention (CPI)	A nonviolent crisis intervention to help reduce the risk of injury to client and staff.
Deprivation	The absence of reduction of a reinforcer for a period of time. Deprivation is an establishing operation that increases the effectiveness of the reinforcer and the rate of behavior that produced that reinforcer in the past.
Differential Reinforcement of Alternative Behaviors (DRA)	Reinforcement of a more appropriate form of a targeted behavior (ask instead of demand something), for example, clinician can present break icon instead of tantrum.
Differential Reinforcement of Higher Rates of Behaviors (DRH)	Reinforces the small increases in the rate of behavior, for example, if a child doesn't want to try a new food, he or she takes one bite and gets reward, etc.
Differential Reinforcement of Incompatible Behaviors (DRI)	Reinforces behaviors that are different from, or incompatible with, the target behavior, for example, if child is constantly touching neighbors, reinforce for having hands in lap.

ABA Terms	Definition
Differential Reinforcement of Low Rates of Behavior (DRL)	Reinforces behaviors if a specified period of time has elapsed since the behavior last occurred, or if there have been only a specified number of episodes during a particular interval, for example, when a child stands up 10 times in an hour, reinforce when only standing 5 times, etc.
Differential Reinforcement of Other Behaviors (DRO)	Reinforces any behavior other than the target behavior for a specific interval of time, for example, if a child hits, reward for any behavior other than when the child hits.
Discrete Trial Training (DTT)	Tasks are broken down into short simple tasks. Single cycle of behavioral-based instructional routine consisting of a question (SD), followed by response or a behavior, followed by a reinforcer (praise, edible).
Discriminative Stimulus (SD)	The command given to the client (show me, point to, where is etc.).
Distractor Trial	When there is more than one choice offered during a trial, for example, asking the child to point to red when there are other "distractor" choices offered such as another color,
Echolalia	Repetition or echoing of verbal utterances made by another person.
Emotional Regulation	The child's ability to notice and respond to internal and external sensory input, and then adjust his or her emotions and behavior to the demands of the surroundings.
Event Recording	An observational recording procedure in which the number of occurrences of a given discrete behavior are counted—number of times correct answers are given, blows delivered, and so on—over a specified period of time.
Exclusion Time-Out	Physical removal of student from a reinforcing environment or activity for a period of time.
Expressive Language	The use of verbal behavior or speech to communicate thoughts, ideas, and feelings with others.
Extinction	Gradually reduces the frequency or intensity of a target behavior by withholding reinforcement from a behavior that was previously reinforced, for example, if John sends 100 emails a day to Sandy, but Sandy doesn't respond to any of the emails, the frequency of John's emails will reduce due to extinction.
Extinction Burst	The increase in frequency and/or intensity of a behavior in the early stages of extinction.
Fading	Gradual removal of prompts.

ABA Terms	Definition
Fine-Motor Skills	Activities that require the coordination of the smaller muscles of the body such as the hand.
Fixed Interval Schedule of Reinforcement	Reinforced after a fixed amount of time has passed, for example, rewarded every 5 minutes.
Fixed Ratio Schedule of Reinforcement	Reinforced after a fixed number of responses occur, for example, rewarded every 5 times the student does a task.
Function	Why a behavior occurs (escape, attention seeking, gain access, self-stimulatory).
Functional Analysis Assessment	Documenting a functional relationship between the occurrence of a problem behavior, antecedent, and consequence events through direct observation and the manipulation of environmental events.
Functional Behavior Analysis (FBA)	A collection of different procedures of gathering information on antecedents, behaviors, and consequences in order to determine the factors that led to and maintains problem behavior.
Functionally Equivalent Replacement Behavior (FERB)	An alternative, acceptable behavior that serves the same purpose for a child, for example, teaching him or her to apply pressure to a face instead of slapping a face.
Generalization	The use of newly learned skills in a setting that is different than the setting in which the skill was initially learned.
Gross-Motor Skills	Activities we do using our larger muscle groups, such as sitting, walking, and jumping.
Individualized Education Plan (IEP)	A legal document that describes the individualized curriculum plan that school-age children have if they are in special education.
Intraverbal	A type of language that involves explaining, discussing, or describing an item or situation that is not present, or not currently happening, for example, answering, "How are you?"
Mand	When a child requests or demands something.
Mass Trial	Only one choice offered during a trial, for example, asking the child to point to red and only holding red out as a choice.
Modeling	Demonstrating or showing a task or behavior.
Natural Antecedents	Events or situations that should act as natural prompts or cues for specific behavior, for example, teachers whisper when they want the class to quiet down.

ABA Terms	Definition
Natural Reinforcer	When the reinforcement happens in a natural setting versus a table top setting, for example, kisses, hugs, tickles, etc.
Negative Punishment	The taking away of something to decrease a certain behavior, for example, a teenager comes home after curfew and the parents take away the cell phone. The frequency of the teenager coming home late will decrease, making the removal of the phone a negative punishment.
Negative Reinforcement	The taking away of an aversive stimulus to increase a certain behavior or response, for example, the sound a car makes when the seat belt is off is aversive. If the behavior of wearing a seatbelt increases, the beeping sound the car made was a negative reinforcement.
Non-Exclusion Time-Out	Student not removed from the reinforcing environment, but attention or other reinforcements are taken from the student for a limited amount of time.
Operant Conditioning	A method of learning or behavior change that occurs through reward or punishment.
Overcorrection	Repeated practice of an appropriate behavior, for example, practice walking in the hallway without touching people over and over.
Perseveration	Repeating or getting stuck carrying out a behavior when it is no longer appropriate.
Pivotal Response Training (PRT)	Child-led, play-based format to develop pivotal skills. Emphasizes turn-taking, child choice, modeling, shaping, and direct reinforcement.
Planned Ignoring	Removal of social reinforcers, such as attention, verbal, or physical interaction.
Positive Punishment	The adding of something to decrease a certain behavior or response, for example, a mother yells at her child when he or she runs into the street. If the running into the street decreases, the yelling is a positive punishment.
Positive Reinforcement	The adding of something to increase a certain behavior or response, for example, a father gives candy to his daughter when she cleans up her toys. If the frequency of picking up the toys increases, the candy is a positive reinforcement.
Preference Assessment	Used to determine the reinforcer that a person prefers.
Primary Learning Channels	Visual and auditory that allow us to learn about our environment.
Priming	A strategy used to help prepare the child for an upcoming event.
Progress Report	The document containing the goals for the client and the graphs representing the data that was collected by the clinician.

ABA Terms	Definition
Prompt	A hint or reminder designed to obtain a desired response. Can be verbal, physical, gestural, visual, and/or modeling.
Prosody	The rhythm and melody of spoken language expressed through rate, pitch, stress, inflection, or intonation.
Psychophysiology	The study of the relationship between physiological and psychological.
Random Rotation	Similar to distractor trial, but the choices are rotated, for example, a child is asked to point to red and there is a blue, red, and orange card on the table. Clinicians can rotate the location of the red card each time they ask the child to point to red.
Rapid Prompting Method	A "teach-ask" paradigm for eliciting responses. The teacher matches his or her pace to the student's speed of self-stimulatory behavior, while continuously speaking and requesting student responses, in order to keep the student on task and focused on the lesson.
Receptive Language	The ability to understand or comprehend words and sentences that others use.
Response Block	A positive punishment technique that is used to prevent a child from emitting problem behavior, for example, blocking a child from continuing to throw toys.
Response Cost	Taking away a specific amount of reinforcers after each problem behavior, for example, taking away tokens, toys, or minutes of computer time.
Rituals	Specific and seemingly meaningless behaviors that a child performs repeatedly in certain situations or circumstances, such as turning the lights on and off several times when entering a room.
Satiation	Excessive use, consumption, or repetition of a behavior, the reinforcer then loses its effectiveness.
Scatterplot	An interval recording method where data are recorded during specific time or activity periods.
Schedule of Reinforcement	A rule specifying the environmental arrangements and response requirements for reinforcement.
Scripting	When a child engages in a verbal stim where he or she repeats or "scripts" phrases or entire sections of a TV show, movie, commercial, etc.
Secondary Learning Channels	Tactile and kinesthetic that allow us to manipulate our environment.

ABA Terms	Definition
Setting Events	Any occurrence that affects a student's responses to reinforcers and punishers in the environment. Setting events can be due to environmental, social, or physiological factors.
Shaping	Teaches gradual approximations of a target behavior, for example, teaching someone to put an arm into the shirt when trying to teach a child to dress themselves. The child would then move on to the next step until he or she eventually learns the entire process of putting on a shirt.
Social Reciprocity	The back-and-forth flow of social interaction. How the behavior of another person influences and is influenced by the behavior of another person and vice versa.
Stimming	Stimulatory behaviors that are self-initiated, repetitive movements that a child might engage in for sensory purposes, and personal enjoyment, for example, rocking, flapping, spinning, finger-flicking, etc.
Stimulus Change	A sudden introduction of an unrelated stimulus that results in a temporary reduction of the behavior, for example, clapping once loudly when a child is having a tantrum.
Successive Approximations	Steps toward the target behavior.
Tact	When a child labels something.
Target Behavior	The behavior being measured, the dependent variable.
Task Analysis	Breaking down a complex skill, job, or behavioral chain into its component behaviors, sub skills, or subtasks.
Time-Out	Temporary separation from the group.
Token	An object that is awarded, contingent on appropriate behavior and that serves as the medium of exchange for backup reinforcers.
Token Economy	A symbolic reinforcement system. Reinforcers that the client earns and can be traded later for something of more value to the client, for example, poker chips awarded for positive behaviors can later be traded for a trip to the movies.
Transition	Moving from one activity or setting to another.
Treatment Plan	The document containing information about the client and the goals of therapy, which are written by a licensed clinician after assessment.
Variable Interval Schedule of Reinforcement	Reinforcement given after an average interval of time, for example, rewarded after 3 minutes, then after 5 minutes, then after 1 minute, etc. This is effective because the student never knows when the reinforcement is going to be given.

ABA Terms	Definition
Variable Ratio Schedule of Reinforcement	Reinforcement given after an average number of responses, for example, a slot machine pays out after a certain number of tries, therefore it is more reinforcing to keep playing on the machine because you never know if your next try will be the winner.
Video Modeling	When desired behaviors are learned by watching a video demonstration and then imitating the behavior of the model.
Visual Motor Integration	Coordinating visual perceptual skills together with gross-motor movement and fine-motor movement. The ability to integrate visual input with motor output.

Levels of Proficiency		
Measure	Definition	Example
Frequency	The number of times a response occurs.	Paula will complete 4 reports. Jake will provide at least 1 answer and 1 question when conversing with peers.
Percentage	Proportion or number of times achieved or correct, divided by total possible times multiplied by 100.	David will complete 90 percent of his assignments this week.
Duration	The length of time that passes from the onset to the offset of a behavior.	Henry will brush his teeth for a full 2 minutes.
Rate	The number of times a response occurs within a given period of time or per opportunity.	John will practice for an hour a day.

Dimensions of Behavior		
Dimensions	Descriptor	Examples
Topography	The form, appearance, or shape of the behavior; its physical or natural features.	Lea is to sit with all 4 legs of the chair on the floor, facing forward, her bottom on the seat, with her feet on the floor.

Accuracy	The extent or degree to which the response meets standards.	Sam will begin to pick up his toys within 2 minutes of his mother saying, "Time to clean up."
Latency	The time that elapses between an antecedent (cue, prompt, signal) and a response.	Sam will begin to pick up his toys within 2 minutes of his mother saying, "Time to clean up."
Intensity	Strength or force with which a behavior is expressed.	Maria will speak loudly enough for all her friends to hear.

Time-Sampling Method		
Interval recording is used for the same behaviors as duration recording, but it takes less time and effort, and does not require that the student be observed continually.		
Method	How to do and Errors	Use Especially When
Whole	Observe the student for a few seconds at designated intervals and notice whether the behavior occurs for the whole interval that you are looking for it (mark "yes" or "no" as to whether this behavior occurred for the whole time that you were watching). Underestimates.	Increasing behavior
Partial	Mark whether the behavior occurred at least once during the short observation interval. Overestimates.	Decreasing behavior
Momentary	Look up immediately at predesignated points and notice whether the behavior is occurring at that precise moment. In all three types, the teacher then figures the percent of observations that the behavior occurred. Random.	

Stimulus Presentation	Target Behavior Increases	Target Behavior Decreases
Stimulus Added	Positive reinforcement	Positive punishment
Stimulus Removed	Negative reinforcement	Negative punishment

Schedules of Reinforcement	Responses	Time
Continuous	Continuous (CRF)	Continuous (CRF)
Fixed	Fixed Ratio (FR)	Fixed Interval (FI)
Variable	Variable Ratio (VR)	Variable Interval (VI)

"Darkness cannot drive out darkness: only light can do that. Hate cannot drive out hate: only love can do that."

— MARTIN LUTHER KING JR.

About the Authors

Jamie L. Melillo, Doctor of Education Candidate, LMFT, PPSC, CWAC, PRTC, Behavior Analyst

Phone: (909) 265-2086 Fax: (909) 989-0456

Website: http://www.hopeforautismfoundation.org

Email: jamie@hopeincca.com

Please visit: http://hopeforautism.tcdmcs.com/

Licensed Marriage Family Therapist
Licensure: February 13, 2007-2017
Board of Behavioral Sciences, 1625 N. Market Blvd., Suite S-200, Sacramento, CA 95834
(916) 574-7830 http://www.bbs.ca.gov

Pupil Personnel Counseling Credential w/ Child Welfare & Attendance Certificate
Validation: January 13, 2016
State of California Commission on Teaching Credential
Email: credentials@ctc.ca.gov

Behavior Analyst Certificate
University of Denver, Colorado
P.O. Box 173364, Denver, CO 80217-3364
(303) 315-6300

Languages
English
Spanish—Conversational Only

***Practice Competencies* (ages 2–18)**
Crisis Management, Autism, ADHD, Anxiety, Bipolar Disorder, Down Syndrome, Depression, EMDR, MR, PTSD, OCD, and Tourette's Syndrome.

Education
September 2016 to present
Berkeley Law Department
UC Berkeley
Berkeley, CA 94720-7200
(510) 642-1741

July 2014 to Current
Global Executive Doctor of Education (EdD)
USC Rossier School of Education
3470 Trousdale Parkway Los Angeles, CA
(213) 740-0224
January 2013 to December 2013 Certified
Behavior Analyst Certificate

University of Denver, Colorado
P.O. Box 173364 Denver, CO 80217-3364
(303) 315-6300

July 2009 to 2011
Doctor of Philosophy in Psychology Candidate (PhD)
Northcentral University
10000 E University Dr., Prescott Valley, AZ 86314, CA
(213) 740-0224; (928) 541-7777

September 11, 2000, to December 14, 2002
MS Counseling (Summa Cum Laude) Pupil
Personnel Counseling Credential

Board Certified Behavioral Analyst (BCBA) Emphasis Child
Welfare & Attendance Certificate (CWAC)
California State University Los Angeles
5151 State University Drive, Los Angeles, CA 90032
(323) 343-4680

September 11, 1995, to September 4, 1998
B.A. Social Work (Cum Laude)
California State University Los Angeles
5151 State University Drive, Los Angeles, CA 90032
(323) 343-4680

Credentials
January 13, 2004, to February 1, 2008
School Counseling: Pupil Personnel Services and School Child
Welfare and Attendance
State of California Commission on Teacher Credentialing #
040097754

Employment History
January 2006 to Current
**Founder & Executive Director of Hope, Inc. Academy 501(c)
(3), Hope, Inc. Institute Nonprofit, & Hope for Autism
Foundation 501(c)(3)**
Duties include: School and Outpatient Mental Health Clinic
providing administrative oversight, psychotherapy, supervision,
advocacy and educational services to children with autism and
other related disabilities. Provide individual and family therapy,
behavioral, and educational trainings, and consultation to local
agencies, private organizations, and public school systems regarding
childhood disorder such as Autism, Asperger's ADHD, Bipolar,
Depression, GAD, ID, and PTSD.

September 2001 to present
President of Melillo Administrative Services
Duties include: Independent contracting services to companies of varies industries providing QuickBooks accounting, payroll services, human resources, business management, advertising, and marketing.

December 2003—January 2007
Village Counseling MFT Intern
Duties: Private practice internship providing educational counseling, individual and family therapy to children, adolescents and adults utilizing cognitive behavioral, strategic, solution focused, and applied behavioral analysis methods.

October 1999 to November 2003
School Counselor & Teacher
Montebello Unified School District, 123 S. Montebello Blvd., Montebello, CA, 90640
(323) 887-7900; San Gabriel Unified School District, 408 Junipero Serra Drive, San Gabriel, CA, 91776, (626) 451-5400; Los Angeles Unified School District and Temple City Unified School District
Duties: maintaining the environment of the classroom, carrying out educational instruction and supervision of children, support services to children with emotional concerns.

January 1995 to September 1999
Senior Tutor and Teacher Internship
California State University Los Angeles, 5151 State University Drive, Los Angeles, CA, 90032, (323) 343-4680
Duties include: Teaching 7th and 8th grade students, program management, educational workshops for Los Angeles Unified School District, supervision for college conferences, administrative duties and promotion.

Volunteer Work
August 2010—present
Autism Alliance Task Force
Sit on committees assisting with the development of Assembly Bills for State Senators impacting children with autism and health care reform. SB946 committee completed.

August 2001—August 2003
California State University Los Angeles, 5151 State University Drive,
Los Angeles, CA, 90032
(323) 343-4680
Marriage Family Therapist Trainee providing therapeutic counseling services to families in a clinical setting.

February 1997—June 1999
Santa Monica Unified School District, 1651 16th Street, Santa Monica, CA, 90404,
(310) 450-8338
Peer Mediation Program provided education programs on conflict resolution and behavioral modification to mid-level students, facilitated peer mediation conferences.

Continuing Education

EMDR Part 1 Basic Training	Biofeedback	Neurofeedback
EMDR Part 11 Training Rating Scales	Mind Your Business Law/ Ethics	Gilliam Autism
Psychotherapeutic Medications Rating Scales	Autism Diagnostic Interview	Gilliam Asperger's
Applied Behavior Analysis Rating Scales	CBT for ADHD	Childhood Autism
Rapid Prompting Method Response Training II	ABA: Pivotal Response Training I	ABA: Pivotal
AAMFT Clinical Supervision Therapy	CAMFT Clinical Supervision	Cognitive Behavioral

Floortime/DIR and RDI	FastForward	Cogmed Working
Brain Gym	Tecademics	Transcendental Meditation

Certifications
Applied Behavioral Analysis: Pivotal Response Training
Certification Level 1 and Level 2
The Koegel Institute at University of California Santa Barbara.

Applied Behavioral Analysis
Continuing Education Unit Provider Board of Behavioral Sciences

Certificate in Behavior Analysis, pending BCBA exam
University of Denver Colorado

Rapid Prompting Method
Halo

Publications
"What Does the Autism Epidemic Mean for Our Profession?"
The Therapist, Journal of California Association of Marriage and Family Therapists

"Applied Behavioral Analysis: Methods and Applications of an Applied Science"
Woman's Symposium, University of Riverside

Domininc Salvatore Juarez

Phone: (909) 265-2086 Fax: (909) 989-0456

Website: http://www.hopeforautismfoundation.org

Email: jamie@hopeincca.com

Languages
Your Child Can Type, Rapid Prompting Method
AAC

Education
Glendora Unified School District 2003-2004 and 2016-present
Unlawfully denied, inaccurately labeled, discriminated against, and abused.

Etiwanda Unified School District 2004-2016
Unlawfully denied, inaccurately labeled, discriminated against, and abused.

Anthem Blue Cross Los Angeles Police Relief Association 2002-present
Unlawfully denied, inaccurately diagnosed, discriminated against, and abused.

Services Received

EMDR Part 1 Basic Training	Biofeedback	Neurofeedback
EMDR Part 11 Training Rating Scales	Mind Your Business Law/ Ethics	Gilliam Autism
Psychotherapeutic Medications Rating Scales	Autism Diagnostic Interview	Gilliam Asperger's
Applied Behavior Analysis Rating Scales	CBT for ADHD	Childhood Autism
Rapid Prompting Method Response Training II	ABA: Pivotal Response Training I	ABA: Pivotal

AAMFT Clinical Supervision Therapy	CAMFT Clinical Supervision	Cognitive Behavioral
Floortime/DIR and RDI	FastForward	Cogmed Working
	Tecademics	Transcendental Meditation
Brain Gym	Tecademics	Transcendental Meditation